A CRITICAL ANALYSIS ON LAW RELATING TO RAPE VICTIMS IN INDIA

SARITA SINGH GAUD

Made with ♥ on the Notion Press Platform
www.notionpress.com

Dedicated to
My Beloved Father
Late Shri. Hari Har Singh

Contents

PREFACE

The issue of sexual violence, particularly rape, remains one of the most pressing and pervasive challenges facing contemporary India. Despite the existence of robust legal frameworks designed to address and mitigate such offenses, survivors of rape often encounter significant obstacles in their pursuit of justice. This book, "A Critical Analysis on Law Relating to Rape Victims in India," delves into the intricacies of the legal system, examining the efficacy of current laws and the systemic barriers that impede the realization of justice for survivors.

The journey towards justice for rape victims in India is fraught with numerous challenges. The transition from the Indian Penal Code (IPC) to the Bharatiya Nyaya Sanhita (BNS) and the Criminal Procedure Code (CrPC) to the Bharatiya Nagarik Suraksha Sanhita (BNSS) reflects efforts to modernize and adapt legal frameworks to better serve the needs of society. These legislative changes aim to strengthen the protection and support for victims, ensuring that their rights and dignity are preserved throughout the legal process. However, the implementation of these laws often falls short due to various systemic issues, including societal stigma, procedural delays, and inadequate sensitivity among law enforcement agencies.

This book provides a comprehensive analysis of the laws relating to rape in India, tracing their evolution, scrutinizing their application, and highlighting the gaps that persist in the system. By examining landmark cases, legislative reforms, and statistical data, this book offers an in-depth understanding of the legal landscape and its impact on rape victims. Additionally, it explores the role of social, cultural, and institutional factors in shaping the experiences of survivors within the judicial system.

Our objective is to shed light on the complexities and nuances of the legal process, advocating for a more empathetic and efficient approach to handling rape cases. By identifying the strengths and weaknesses of existing laws and practices, we aim to contribute to the ongoing discourse on legal reform and gender justice in India. This book is intended for legal professionals, scholars, policymakers, and anyone interested in understanding and addressing the challenges faced by rape victims in their quest for justice.

We hope that this critical analysis will serve as a valuable resource, fostering greater awareness and prompting meaningful changes in the legal and social systems to better support rape survivors and promote gender equality in India.

~ Sarita Singh Gaud

Acknowledgements

The completion of this book, **_"A Critical Analysis on Law Relating to Rape Victims in India,"_** has been a challenging yet profoundly rewarding journey. It would not have been possible without the support, guidance, and encouragement of numerous individuals and institutions.

First and foremost, I express my deepest gratitude to my family for their unwavering support and understanding. Your encouragement and patience have been my pillar of strength throughout this endeavor.

I would like to extend my sincere thanks to my academic mentors and colleagues, whose expertise and insights have been invaluable in shaping this work. My appreciation also goes to the legal professionals, activists, and scholars who provided their time and expertise, offering critical perspectives and feedback. Your contributions have enriched this book, ensuring a comprehensive and nuanced analysis.

Lastly, I am grateful to my friends and peers who offered their support and encouragement along the way. Your belief in my work has been a constant source of motivation.

This book is the result of collective effort and collaboration, and I am deeply thankful to everyone who contributed to its creation. I hope it will serve as a meaningful contribution to the discourse on legal reform and the rights of rape victims in India.

~ Sarita Singh Gaud

List of Abbreviations

NCRB - National Crime Records Bureau

PTSD - Post-traumatic Stress Disorder

FIRs - First Information Reports

NALSA - National Legal Services Authority

VCF - Victim Compensation Fund

CTED - Counter-Terrorism Committee Executive Directorate

IPC - Indian Penal Code

CrPC - Criminal Procedure Code

POSCO - Protection of Children from Sexual Offences

MTP - Medical Termination of Pregnancy

Case Laws

Tukaram v. State of Maharashtra (1979) State of Punjab v. Gurmit Singh (1996) State of Haryana v. Bhajan Lal (1992)

Bodhisattwa Gautam v. Subhra Chakraborty (1996) State of Karnataka v. Krishnappa (2000)

State of Rajasthan v. N.K. (2000)

State of Himachal Pradesh v. Asha Ram (2005) State of Uttar Pradesh v. Chhotey Lal (2008) Bhanwari Devi v. State of Rajasthan (1995)

State of Maharashtra v. Madhukar Narayan Mardikar (1991) Lalita Kumari v. Government of Uttar Pradesh (2013)

State of Punjab v. Ramdev Singh (2004) State of Rajasthan v. Om Prakash (2002) State of Uttar Pradesh v. Man Singh (2010)

Delhi Domestic Working Women's Forum v. Union of India (1995) Vishakha v. State of Rajasthan (1997)

I

Introduction

INTRODUCTION

Rape is one of the most heinous crimes that can be committed, and it carries a social stigma that is often applied directly or indirectly to the victim. There is a lack of satisfaction among rape victims in India due to the difficulties they encounter in our culture. The effects of rape are devastating. For justice to be served, the victim must go through an experience that is eerily similar to the one she went through when the crime was committed. A rape victim faces numerous obstacles on the path to justice. As a member of a poor or marginalised community, she or her family may face significant resistance when attempting even the most basic form of complaint resolution. Services meant to help are also relatively inactive. Thus, a rape victim faces numerous post- incident physical, psychological, and social effects.

The collective consciousness must shift. Assuring the rape victim that it was not her fault and that society stands with her is an essential part of providing the support she needs. As a society, we must do what is necessary to help rape victims[1].

The concept of rape is not foreign to modern culture. Its prevalence spans both antiquity and the modern era. Our culture stigmatises victims who report rape, but the truth is that many rapes go unreported because of this. The shame and humiliation a rape victim experiences when coming forward is almost as bad as the assault itself, with many people assuming that the victim was at fault. The social stigma attached to a single woman makes it difficult for her to find a partner. Moreover, the relatives and close acquaintances of the victim may be hesitant to disclose information about the crime. The survivor of a rape crime may also experience a sense of guilt for having survived the traumatic event. Therefore, it is crucial for our society to implement laws and amend existing ones that not only deliver justice to the victims but also aid them in rebuilding their lives. The authorities and society at large must strive to ensure that the survivor feels safe and comfortable after such an incident.

Roughly one woman is a victim of rape every four minutes in India. The National Crime Records Bureau (NCRB) reported 31,677 cases of rape in 2021 which workout to an average of 86 rape per day in india, Victims of rape suffer adverse effects on multiple levels, including the physiological, psychological, and social. Rape survivors in India face significant obstacles in accessing justice and other services. To say that the situation for rape victims in India is not satisfactory would be an understatement. Not only do women who have been raped have to overcome legal obstacles, but they must also deal with the stigma and hostility of a society that views the issue from a very different angle. I want to state unequivocally that just as people are fleeing the COVID- 19 positive person in the present, so too do people flee the rape victim as if she were the perpetrator.

There's an 82-page report and everyone's pointing fingers at me: According to the report, "Barriers to Justice and Support Services for Sexual Assault Survivors in India," women in India who have survived rape or other sexual offences often face stigma and poor treatment at the hands of the police and medical professionals. Despite the fact that authorities are often reluctant to file complaints and victims and witnesses are sometimes not afforded any protection, doctors often insist that victims submit to "two-finger" tests. In India, survivors of rape face hardships that most Westerners can't even begin to fathom. Everyone in the country was shocked eight years ago when the brutality threshold was breached in the Delhi gang rape case. While rape laws and policies have become more stringent in recent years, police, medical professionals, and the legal system all have a responsibility to treat victims with respect. There are many obstacles that rape victims must overcome before they can receive justice.

The above statement was proclaimed by the doctors involved in the treatment of Nirbhaya, a young woman who was brutally gang-raped on a bus in Delhi. The attack resulted in organ failure and her untimely demise. The incident raises a critical question - do the dignity and life of women hold any value in this country? Unfortunately, in the Nirbhaya case, it took over seven years to deliver justice to the victim.

In a famous case **Rafiq v. State of U.P** "A murderer kills the body but a rapist kills the souls."

"It takes time to change mind-sets, but the Indian government should ensure medical counselling, and legal support to victims and their families, and at the same time do more to sensitize police officers, judicial officials, and medical professionals on the proper handling of sexual violence cases."

Rape and sexual assault affect people of all ages, genders, sexual orientations, races, religions, socioeconomic backgrounds, and abilities. Rape incidents can be broken down into several distinct groups based on factors such as the nature of the relationship between the offender and the victim and the setting in which the assault took place. Date rape, gang rape, marital rape, inconsentual rape, sexual abuse of a child, rape in prison, rape by an acquaintance, rape in war, and statutory rape are all examples. Involuntary sex acts can be carried out repeatedly without causing serious harm.

- **Rape Cases in India**

Here is a table with data on the reported cases of rape in India over the past few years, as per the National Crime Records Bureau (NCRB):

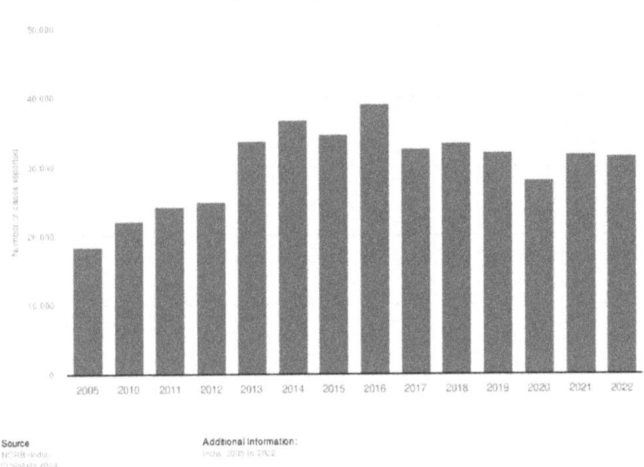

It is important to note that these numbers only represent reported cases, and the actual number of rape incidents is likely much higher due to underreporting and other factors. Additionally, the data only includes reported cases, and not all reported cases may result in charges, convictions, or justice for survivors.

• Background

Since 1860, the laws regarding sexual offences and rape have remained unchanged; it wasn't until the Mathura Rape case that this changed. Protests erupted all over the country after this case's verdict was announced, and the result was a revision of the law.

Following this, the Criminal Law (Amendment) Act of 1983 was enacted, which amended the Indian Evidence Act of 1872 by adding Section 114-A, which provides a presumption of the absence of consent in rape prosecutions if the victim so states[2].

In addition, Section 228-A was added to the Indian Penal Code in 1860, making it illegal to publicly identify victims of certain crimes, such as rape.

After that, the Justice J.S. Verma Committee's report resulted in the Criminal Law (Amendment) Act of 2013. Through this Amendment, the previous minimum age for sexual activity was raised to 18. If you have sexual contact with a girl under the age of 18, with or without her permission, you have committed rape. A girl under the age of 18 cannot legally give her consent to sexual activity. With this change, sexual harassment, voyeurism, and stalking are all considered sexual offences. With this Amendment, new sections were added to the Criminal Law. This Amendment has become the most significant in the history of Criminal Laws, and it has resulted in numerous changes to these laws.

- **Rape Victims Faces Barriers to Justice**

The trauma of sexual assault can alter a woman's outlook on life irrevocably. There have been periodic updates to the law to reflect societal shifts, including the introduction and revision of new gender-related statutes. Following the Nirbhaya Case and the recommendation of the Justice JS Verma Committee, the major change was implemented in 2013. The scope of "Sex Crimes" was broadened by this 2013 amendment. We now include Sexual Harassment, Voyeurism, and Stalking under the umbrella term Sexual Offenses. The acts listed above carried no consequences prior to the passing of this

Amendment. Several reports indicated that the investigation into the case and the filing of charge sheets took too long. The victim or their family members report feeling threatened by the accused after filing a complaint against the crime because the accused is granted bail so quickly. Despite the necessity, victims of rape often do not receive adequate protection during ongoing trials.

Additionally, it has come to light that law enforcement and other supporting authorities may not take rape crimes seriously, particularly if the victim is a girl or woman from a lower social class. In a landmark ruling, the Supreme Court directed the Police to provide legal aid to victims of sexual assault and maintain a list of legal aid options. However, survivors from marginalized and impoverished communities still lack sufficient legal assistance due to a lack of awareness of their rights. Although federal and state governments have implemented various measures to aid survivors of sexual assault, these efforts have not been effectively monitored or evaluated, leading to a failure to achieve their intended objectives.[3].

We hope that the victims will be able to use the resources we provide to help them recover from the tragedy they have experienced and move on with their lives. The stigma attached to speaking out about rape needs to be reduced significantly.

The primary barriers which are faced by a victim of rape are:

i. Difficulty in Register Complaints: -Particularly challenging is the process of filing a complaint on behalf of survivors or victims who come from socially excluded groups. Human Rights Watch also discovered that crime victims in India were reluctant to come forward for fear of retaliation from the accused and the ineffectiveness of the justice system.

ii. Suffers Humiliation: -Victims of rape are often made to feel bad by people who are supposed to help them. This includes police officers and doctors, who, even after the Supreme Court's rules, still use humiliating tests like the "two-finger" test. Rape is a crime against women, but in our culture, women are treated as if they did the crime. Rape is still seen as a source of shame for women, and women don't feel comfortable talking about it.

iii. Poor Police Response: - Unfortunately, the Police Authorities do not always adhere to the regulations which are specified by the statutes. The victim's family may feel pressure from law enforcement to reach a settlement or make a concession.

iv. Fourthly, the failure to provide access to adequate healthcare services is a significant concern. In 2014, the Ministry of Health and Family Welfare released guidelines for medico-legal care aimed at standardizing the examination and treatment of survivors of sexual violence in healthcare settings. However, there are still challenges in ensuring that such victims receive comprehensive and appropriate medical attention. These recommendations provide more reliable scientific medical data and put an end to harmful myths like the two-finger test by restricting them to internal vaginal examinations. Health care, however, is a matter that falls under state jurisdiction in India's federal structure, so individual state governments are not required to implement these policies. Just a handful of states have followed these recommendations so far.

v. Lack of access to effective Legal Assistance: - Those survivors who are low- income or otherwise marginalised face additional challenges due to a lack of adequate legal representation. No one has informed them of their right to free legal representation. The Supreme Court declared that victims of sexual assault must be given access to legal representation in 1994, and it is the responsibility of police to maintain a directory of available legal aid resources in every police station.

vi. Lack of Support Services: - To evaluate the efficacy of laws prohibiting violence against women in India, there is no such nationwide monitoring and appraisal structure. The Central Government established the Nirbhaya Fund in 2013 to aid in the prevention, protection, and rehabilitation of female victims of rape. There are numerous other schemes intended to achieve this goal, but they suffer from a lack of coordination and public awareness[4].

- **EFFECTS OF RAPE ON VICTIMS**

Rape is such a traumatic experience which leaves many impacts on the victims physical as well as psychological. The impacts which a victim may go through are:

A. Psychological Impact:

- "Immediate effect – the survivors or victims usually have fear, scary thoughts and nightmares followed by the incidence.
- Anxiety – they have high level of anxiety or phobia after the attack. They often also have the feeling of nervousness, uneasiness, dread or may have panic attacks.
- Hyper sexuality – this is also one of the impact on victim.

- ○ Post-traumatic Stress Disorder- The National Victim Centre and the Crime Victim's Research and Treatment Centre released a report which have finding that 31% of the woman after the incidence at some faces PTSD.
- ○ Depression

- ○ Self-Blame – it causes in victim lack of motivation, empathy, feeling of isolation, anger, aggression etc.
- ○ Suicide – survivors of rape are more likely to commit rape because they feel embarrassed about the victim, have feeling of self-blame".

B. Physical Impact:

- ○ Gynaecological effects – like survivors suffer vaginal bleeding or infection, vaginitis inflammation, chronic pelvic pain, urinary tract infection etc.
- ○ Pregnancy
- ○ Sexually Transmitted Diseases

C. Sociological impact and mistreatment of victims

Investigations into sexual assault often result in further mistreatment of victims. Victims' right to privacy is violated and her credibility is called into question while the case is being tried. Victims of sexual assault often suffer additional harms, such as secondary victimisation and self-blame.

- Secondary Victimisation – Rape is a taboo topic because of the social stigma attached to it. A rape victim, for instance, is viewed as flawed by the community. They may be rejected by their friends and family, feel alone, have trouble getting married, or be divorced by their husbands. We call this phenomenon "secondary victimisation".

- Self-Blaming – In this case, "blaming" means making the victim responsible for the crime. For example, society has different ideas about how a rape victim should act with men and how she should dress, among other things. All of these things can make the victim think that the crime was her fault.

- **Types of Relationship Between Rapist & Victim**

It's important to note that rape is a violent crime that is never the fault of the victim. It is a violation of one's body and autonomy. In terms of relationships between rapists and victims, there are several possible scenarios:

- **Stranger rape:** Stranger rape is a type of sexual assault that occurs when the victim is attacked by someone they do not know. It is a violent crime that can happen to anyone, regardless of their gender, age, or background. In this type of rape, the perpetrator may choose their victim randomly or may stalk them prior to the attack. Stranger rape can happen in a variety of locations, including public spaces, homes, and workplaces. Victims of stranger rape often experience intense feelings of fear, shock, and disbelief. They may feel violated, humiliated, and traumatized. In addition to physical injuries, such as bruises, cuts, and broken bones, victims of stranger rape may also suffer from emotional trauma, including anxiety, depression, and post-traumatic stress disorder (PTSD). Perpetrators of stranger rape may use physical force or weapons to overpower their victims, or they may use drugs or alcohol to incapacitate them.

Some may also use psychological tactics, such as intimidation or manipulation, to control their victims. Perpetrators of stranger rape are often serial offenders, meaning they have raped or attempted to rape multiple people.While stranger rape is a relatively rare type of rape compared to other forms, it is important to acknowledge its impact on victims and society as a whole. It is a crime that violates a person's sense of safety and security in their own community, and can have long-lasting effects on their physical, emotional, and mental well-being.

Preventing stranger rape requires a combination of individual and societal efforts. Individuals can take steps to protect themselves, such as avoiding isolated areas, traveling in groups, and being aware of their surroundings. Society can work to address the root causes of rape, such as toxic masculinity, rape culture, and unequal power dynamics between men and women. Education and awareness campaigns can also help to challenge harmful beliefs and behaviors that contribute to the perpetration of sexual violence.

- **Acquaintance rape:** Acquaintance rape, also known as date rape, is a type of sexual assault that occurs when the victim is assaulted by someone they know. The perpetrator may be a friend, acquaintance, coworker, or romantic partner of the victim. Acquaintance rape is a complex issue that often involves issues of consent, power dynamics, and social norms. One of the key characteristics of acquaintance rape is that the victim and perpetrator have some kind of pre-existing relationship. This can make it difficult for victims to come forward and report the assault, as they may feel ashamed or embarrassed about what happened, or worry about how others will perceive them. Perpetrators of acquaintance rape may also use the victim's trust and familiarity to their advantage, using coercion, manipulation, or other forms of pressure to obtain sexual contact. Acquaintance rape can take many different forms. For example, it may involve the perpetrator taking advantage of a victim who is intoxicated or under the influence of drugs, or it may involve the perpetrator ignoring the victim's verbal or non-verbal cues that they do not want to engage in sexual activity. In some cases, acquaintance rape may involve physical violence or the use of weapons.

- **Intimate partner rape:** Intimate partner rape is a type of sexual assault that occurs when the perpetrator is a current or former romantic partner, spouse, or significant other of the victim. This type of rape is a serious violation of trust, intimacy, and personal boundaries. Intimate partner rape is often underreported and misunderstood, as victims may struggle with feelings of shame, guilt, or fear of retaliation. Perpetrators of intimate partner rape may use a variety of tactics to gain control and power over their victims. This can include physical force, coercion, manipulation, or emotional abuse. Intimate partner rape can take many different forms, including forced sexual activity, sexual touching without consent, or sexual activity under duress. Victims of intimate partner rape may experience a range of emotions, including fear, shame, guilt, and confusion. They may also experience physical injuries, such as bruises, cuts, and broken bones, as well as emotional trauma, such as anxiety, depression, and PTSD. In some cases, intimate partner rape may be part of a larger pattern of abuse, including physical, emotional, and financial abuse. One of the unique challenges of intimate partner rape is that the perpetrator and victim may share a living space, social network, or financial resources. This can make it difficult for victims to seek help or leave the abusive situation. In some cases, victims may also struggle with feelings of loyalty or love towards their abuser, or may worry about the impact of leaving on their children or other family members.

- **Date rape:** Date rape, also known as acquaintance rape, is a type of sexual assault that occurs during a social interaction or date. In this type of rape, the victim is assaulted by someone they know, such as a friend, acquaintance, or romantic partner. Date rape is a serious crime that can have lasting effects on the victim's physical, emotional, and mental health. Date rape can happen in a variety of situations, such as on a first date, during a party, or in a casual social setting. Perpetrators of date rape may use a variety of tactics to gain control over the victim, including coercion, manipulation, or force. They may also use drugs or alcohol to incapacitate the victim, making it easier for them to commit the assault. One of the key characteristics of date rape is that the victim may not initially recognize that they are being assaulted. The perpetrator may use subtle tactics, such as ignoring the victim's boundaries or insisting on sexual activity despite the victim's protests. In some cases, the victim may be too intoxicated or impaired to give clear consent, or may be unaware of what is happening due to their level of intoxication. Victims of date rape may experience a range of emotions, including fear, shame, guilt, and confusion. They may also experience physical injuries, such as bruises, cuts, and broken bones, as well as emotional trauma, such as anxiety, depression, and PTSD. In some cases, date rape may be part of a larger pattern of abuse, including physical, emotional, and financial abuse. Preventing date rape requires a comprehensive response from individuals and society as a whole. This includes increasing education and awareness around healthy relationships and consent, as well as addressing the root causes of gender-based violence and inequality. Providing access to resources and support for victims of date rape is also crucial, as it can help individuals to heal from the trauma and seek justice. It's important to note that regardless of the relationship between the rapist and the victim, rape is a serious crime and should be reported to the authorities immediately.

- **Sexual harassment:** Sexual harassment refers to unwelcome behavior of a sexual nature that creates an intimidating, hostile, or offensive work, academic, or social environment. It can take many forms, including verbal or physical conduct, visual images, or written communications. Sexual harassment is a form of gender-based violence and a violation of human rights, and it can have serious negative impacts on the mental and physical well-being of victims.

Examples of sexual harassment include unwanted touching or physical contact, sexual comments or jokes, unwanted sexual advances or propositions, displaying sexual images or content, or making threats or promises in exchange for sexual favors. It can occur in many different contexts, such as the workplace, schools or universities, public places, or online.

Sexual harassment is a pervasive problem that affects people of all genders, although women are disproportionately impacted. It can have serious negative consequences for victims, including anxiety, depression, PTSD, and other mental health issues, as well as physical health problems such as headaches, stomachaches, and sleep disturbances. It can also impact a victim's professional or academic success, causing them to miss out on opportunities or drop out of school or work.

Preventing and addressing sexual harassment requires a comprehensive response from individuals, organizations, and society as a whole. This includes increasing education and awareness about healthy relationships and consent, promoting workplace and school policies that prohibit sexual harassment and provide support for victims, empowering victims to come forward and report sexual harassment, and holding perpetrators accountable for their actions. It also involves challenging harmful gender norms and stereotypes that contribute to the normalization of sexual harassment in our society. sexual harassment is a serious problem that can have lasting negative impacts on victims. By increasing education and awareness, promoting policies that prohibit sexual harassment and provide support for victims, and challenging harmful gender norms and stereotypes, we can work towards a world where sexual harassment is no longer tolerated or normalized.

- **Sexual Violence and Impunity in India**

Sexual Violence and Impunity in India" is a critical analysis of the legal framework, cultural norms, and socio-political structures that contribute to the pervasive problem of sexual violence and impunity in India. The book by Madhu Kishwar explores the historical, cultural, and political factors that have normalized sexual violence in India and the legal and policy responses to the problem. It analyzes the various provisions of the law relating to sexual offenses and critiques their effectiveness in protecting women and promoting gender justice.

This research also highlights the experiences of marginalized communities, such as Dalit and Adivasi women, and their disproportionate vulnerability to sexual violence. Through a feminist lens, the book provides a nuanced analysis of the complexities of sexual violence in India and advocates for a comprehensive and intersectional approach to addressing the issue. It argues that legal reform alone is not sufficient to address the problem and that broader social and cultural changes, including education and awareness-raising efforts, are necessary to challenge harmful attitudes and norms that perpetuate violence against women.

II
Literature Review

- **Related Work**

Indumathi M J & Dr. M . Suresh Benjamin,(2021) The current legal system does not address the issue of rape within marriage. The incidence of marital rape in India has increased over the past two to three decades, despite the country's growing awareness of its many penal laws. In India, a specialised law against domestic violence is required. However, while many people may disagree with the concept of marital law, few would argue that making marital law a criminal matter would undermine the institution of marriage or that the courts have any business meddling in the private lives of a husband and wife. Women have the right to seek legal protection, but her husband, in whom she placed complete trust when they wed, is trying to harm and torture her by having sexual relations with her against her will, which is detrimental to her health. Aside from being the primary issue in women's rights right now, marital rape also breaches multiple clauses of the constitution. Someone once observed, correctly, that one way to measure a nation's progress is by how it treats its women[5].

Kamthan, M (2018) Feminism, at this pivotal juncture, needs to rethink its relationship to the language of rights and the law. This past decade's events have done more than just cast doubt on the law's ability to be a transformative instrument; they also suggest that operating in a manner compatible with legal discourse may have the potential to radically refract feminism's ethical and liberatory impulse. The intersection of the law and sexuality is a source of growing unease among feminists. In order to free the law's innate justice from the biases of individuals, it is necessary to recognise that the law's inability to deliver justice in feminist terms is a direct result of the law being interpreted in sexist ways. The common understanding of a word is subject to change as a result of shifting social norms and globalisation. More vigilance on the part of the courts is required to ensure that justice is seen to be done, rather than thwarted by the letter of the law, in a country plagued by misconceptions about rape and rape victims, corrupt and sloppy police work, widespread reports of police mistreatment of victims, including custodial rape, and deeply ingrained cultural and religious stereotypes. If rape laws are to serve as a deterrent, many reforms must be made in the courts and the legislature[6].

Rajeev Ranjan, Tanya Grover (2018) A rape is a horrifying and intrusive crime. The victim's life could be irrevocably altered as a result. The victim of some crimes can move on with their lives once the crime itself is over. But rape victims don't have this luxury. Following the conclusion of the attack, the victim will face a wide range of additional difficulties. Long-term effects of sexual assault are felt by many survivors. The assault could result in real bodily harm. It's possible there'll be repercussions on an emotional level, too. It can be difficult for survivors of rape to get back to living normally. They may be showing signs of rape trauma syndrome, a PTSD subtype. Crime patterns in India have shifted as a result of recent sociopolitical shifts and the clash between the ideas of younger and older generations. Men and women alike, not just the police, must shoulder the duty of keeping women safe. If society is to stop stigmatising those who have been raped, it is not enough to simply pass new laws. Though legislation was likely strengthened in the wake of the incident, the incident rate continues to rise due to a lack of effective enforcement[7].

Sakshi Rewaria (2019) Offenses of a sexual nature, such as rape, are of a different nature than other crimes and are the result of a sick mindset. Violent predators are typically sadistic people with a history of criminal behaviour. In many cases, the victim of a rape experiences intense fear and shame as a direct result of the violent crime. It's a violent attack on the woman, her loved ones, and the entire community. Sexual violence, especially rape, is a worldwide epidemic that affects people of all cultures and socioeconomic backgrounds, but is especially pervasive among young people. Most developing nations ignore sexual assault as a public health problem. The Latin root of 'rape', 'rapio,' means to seize. To "ravish" a woman without her consent through the use of force, fear, or deception is to commit the crime of rape, which is also known as "carnal knowledge of a woman, by force against her will." Roughly speaking, rape refers to the carnal knowledge of a woman over a certain age against her will, or a girl or young woman under that age, with or without her consent[8].

Jhanwar, M. (2021) The paper compares and critically evaluates rape laws in India before and after the Criminal Law Amendment Act of 2013. This amendment introduced several new sexual offences and increased punishments and penalties to address the rising incidents of sexual offences against women in Indian cities. However, some provisions may not provide victims of this heinous crime with the full measure of justice they deserve. Furthermore, certain issues that have been neglected to date must be addressed immediately to ensure effective and fair implementation of these laws.The commentary on rape in India has been so gruesome that Delhi has been dubbed the "Rape Capital." Furthermore, male rape statistics were not included in the calculations that resulted in this label for the city. While we celebrate India's comparatively low divorce rate, we fail to recognise the prevalence of domestic violence or the need to make marital rape a criminal offence. Our current sociopolitical system and the gaps in the Indian criminal justice system need fixing before we can effectively combat these unspeakably horrible crimes[9].

Chakraborty, A. (2014) The most abhorrent of all crimes, rape, persists in modern society. Despite numerous protests and the passage of a new law in response to the Delhi gang rape case, nothing has changed. A photojournalist in Mumbai was recently the victim of sexual assault. When reporters from a major newspaper chain travelled to her neighbourhood to conduct an interview, they discovered that no one living in the survivor apartment knew she was a local. In light of this, one might wonder why, years later, the rape survivor continues to feel shame and opts to remain silent. This is a major reason why most rape victims do not report the crime. They fear for her reputation and the rest of her life if the public finds out about this. This is why so-called "modern" society still has problems with rape[10].

G.S. Bajpai and Shriya Gauba (2016) When one person violates the rights of another, the traditional system focuses on criminal behaviour, while restorative justice focuses

on right violations. Unlike the traditional system, which focuses on finding blame, "restorative justice" looks beyond that to the offender's ability to make amends and to the prevention of similar crimes in the future. Unlike the adversarial system, which is burdened by red tape and delays, the justice system is a more streamlined, less bureaucratic way of dealing with legal disputes. The traditional antagonistic system cared little for interpersonal dynamics. However, restorative justice aims to restore harmony between parties. In the old system, only a small number of people would have their interests considered, but in restorative justice, everyone who has a stake in the case would be involved. In contrast to the other system, which treats victims as mere witnesses, victims are at the centre of the restorative justice framework[11].

Pratiksha Baxi, (2014) The government has a strong belief in criminal penalties. If the accused is sent to prison, he will be isolated from other people. In the traditional system, the victim is not physically absent but psychologically distant because he is reduced to a helpless witness whom everyone blames and shames. If the state believes the crime was committed against the state, it will lead the prosecution in an adversarial system. It dispenses justice with the aid of an impartial arbiter of the law called a judge. The state's attorney and the defence attorney both work on the case. Assumptions made on the accused's behalf cause the scales to tip in his favour. Contrarily, the victim's question is addressed by the informal justice system. A societal perspective is also included. The crime in

India is seen as an attack on the state, while in the other system, the offender has violated the victim's rights[12].

Dipa Dube (2018) Broadcast, print, and online news outlets, as well as social media platforms, provided crucial coverage and reporting of the situation, as well as reactions and comments from people all over the country and the world. This not only educated the public, but also infuriated them, leading to unprecedented social support in the form of a nationwide mass movement marked by a candle march, slogan shouting, and a demand for immediate action against the attackers, and involving corporate organisations, schools and colleges, boys and girls, working professionals, housewives, and the common man. The Latin root of rape means "to take" or "to seize." One or more people initiate sexual contact with another person without that person's consent, which on right violations. Unlike the traditional system, which focuses on finding blame, "restorative justice" looks beyond that to the offender's ability to make amends and to the prevention of similar crimes in the future. Unlike the adversarial system, which is burdened by red tape and delays, the justice system is a more streamlined, less bureaucratic way of dealing with legal disputes. The traditional antagonistic system cared little for interpersonal dynamics. However, restorative justice aims to restore harmony between parties. In the old system, only a small number of people would have their interests considered, but in restorative justice, everyone who has a stake in the case would be involved. In contrast to the other system, which treats victims as mere witnesses, victims are at the centre of the restorative justice framework[11].

Pratiksha Baxi, (2014) The government has a strong belief in criminal penalties. If the accused is sent to prison, he will be isolated from other people. In the traditional system, the victim is not physically absent but psychologically distant because he is reduced to a helpless witness whom everyone blames and shames. If the state believes the crime was committed against the state, it will lead the prosecution in an adversarial system. It dispenses justice with the aid of an impartial arbiter of the law called a judge. The state's attorney and the defence attorney both work on the case. Assumptions made on the accused's behalf cause the scales to tip in his favour. Contrarily, the victim's question is addressed by the informal justice system. A societal perspective is also included. The crime in India is seen as an attack on the state, while in the other system, the offender has violated the victim's rights[12].

Dipa Dube (2018) Broadcast, print, and online news outlets, as well as social media platforms, provided crucial coverage and reporting of the situation, as well as reactions and comments from people all over the country and the world. This not only educated the public, but also infuriated them, leading to unprecedented social support in the form of a nationwide mass movement marked by a candle march, slogan shouting, and a demand for immediate action against the attackers, and involving corporate organisations, schools and colleges, boys and girls, working professionals, housewives, and the common man. The Latin root of rape means "to take" or "to seize." One or more people initiate sexual contact with another person without that person's consent, which is why rape is defined as "sexual assault usually involving sexual intercourse." As stated in Section 375 of the Indian Penal Code, "intentional, unlawful sexual intercourse with a woman without her consent" constitutes the crime of rape in India. Some have argued that this definition is too limited because it does not account for other types of sexual assault[13].

Michaela Lehner-Zimmerer (2011), As he explains in his article "Future Challenges of International Victimology," victimology is a field that spans national boundaries. There is a summary of various treaties and agreements made on a global scale. It explains why and how developed and developing countries can benefit from working together internationally. It also recommends that countries establish victim funds in accordance with the United Nations Victim Declaration. There should be an emphasis on victimology studies with these funds. Experts in the field need to work on creating new theories[14].

jhalak Kakkar and Shruti Ojha (2009) It was reported after the attack that the suspects were arrested by police within 24 hours. The five adult males and one juvenile all had alcohol in their systems when they were caught (under 18 years). Since the men didn't have permission to pick up passengers, they were operating the bus illegally. The carpenter, who had boarded the bus thinking it was a scheduled bus, had been robbed by the gang before the rape occurred[15].

Dr. Tiwari J.K. (2014), Many seminal rulings concerning victims have been discussed in "Judicial Attitude Towards Justice of Victims." This demonstrates that the victim must not be ignored in the Indian criminal justice system. When deciding on monetary damages, the judicial system has adopted a practical stance. There are no corresponding legal mandates. Legislative confidence will help the administration of justice. The accused will feel financial pressure to compensate, and crime will go down as a result. Articles, circulars, orders, and case laws pertaining to victims and compensation have been published by the Jharkhand State Legal Services Authority (2016) in the book

"Compendium on Compensatory Relief to the Victims of Crime in the Criminal Justice System[16].

V. N. Ranjan (2012) The victim's plight in India is discussed in the book "***Victimology in India***." He has talked about compensation programmes in other countries in the preceding chapters. Prevention of crime is stressed as he speaks on the topic. If the perpetrator doesn't pay up, he suggests "attachment and sale of property by the Government[17].

Chakraborty, T. (2019). This paper discusses the historical and cultural factors that have contributed to the problem of sexual violence in India and examines the various laws, policies, and guidelines that have been enacted to address the issue. It also provides a critical analysis of the implementation and enforcement of these laws, highlighting the challenges and gaps in the legal framework. The book further explores the role of the judiciary, law enforcement agencies, and other stakeholders in addressing sexual violence and provides recommendations for strengthening the legal framework and improving the justice system for victims of sexual violence. Overall, the book provides a valuable resource for scholars, legal professionals, policymakers, and activists working towards ending sexual violence in India[18].

Jayakumar, V. (2019).This paper provides an in-depth analysis of the legal provisions, judicial practices, and socio-cultural factors that influence rape trials in India. It critically examines the various challenges and barriers faced by victims of sexual violence in accessing justice, including victim-blaming, social stigma, and legal loopholes. The book also explores the role of the police, judiciary, and other stakeholders in the criminal justice system in addressing sexual violence, and provides recommendations for improving the legal framework and justice system for rape victims. Through a combination of legal analysis and empirical research, the book provides a valuable resource for scholars, legal professionals, policymakers, and activists working towards ending sexual violence and improving the justice system for victims of sexual violence in India[19].

Jaising, I. (2013). It analyzes the various provisions of the law relating to rape and sexual offenses and critiques their effectiveness in protecting women and promoting gender justice. The book also explores the intersectional nature of sexual violence, including the experiences of marginalized communities such as Dalit women and transgender individuals, and the need for legal reform to address these issues. Through a combination of legal analysis and advocacy, the book provides a valuable resource for scholars, legal professionals, policymakers, and activists working towards ending sexual violence and promoting gender justice in India[20].

Kishwar, M. (2014). "Sexual Violence and Impunity in India: A Feminist Perspective" by Madhu Kishwar provides a feminist perspective on the pervasive problem of sexual violence and impunity in India. The book analyzes the historical, cultural, and political factors that have contributed to the normalization of sexual violence in India and the legal and policy responses to the problem. It critiques the patriarchal structures and gender biases that have led to a culture of victim-blaming and stigmatization of rape survivors, as well as the inadequate legal framework for addressing sexual violence. The book also highlights the experiences of marginalized communities, such as Dalit and Adivasi women, and their disproportionate vulnerability to sexual violence. Through a feminist lens, the book provides a nuanced analysis of the complexities of sexual violence in India and advocates for a comprehensive and intersectional approach to addressing the issue. The book concludes with recommendations for legal reform, policy changes, and social transformation aimed at ending sexual violence and promoting gender equality in India[21].

Kotwal, V. (2019). The article examines the history of rape laws in India and the key legal provisions related to rape and sexual offenses. It also explores the socio-cultural factors that contribute to sexual violence in India and the challenges faced by victims in accessing justice. Through a critical analysis of the legal framework, the article highlights the gaps and weaknesses in the legal system and the need for legal reforms to ensure justice for rape victims. The article also emphasizes the importance of addressing the structural factors that perpetuate sexual violence, including gender inequality, patriarchal attitudes, and social norms that condone violence against women. The article concludes with a call to action for legal professionals, policymakers, and civil society to work together to improve the legal framework and ensure that rape victims receive justice and support. Overall, the article provides a valuable resource for understanding the legal landscape of rape in India and the need for comprehensive legal and social reforms to address this critical issue[22].

Mehta, A. (2018). The book examines the historical and cultural factors that contribute to sexual violence in India and the various legal and policy responses to the problem. It also explores the challenges and barriers faced by rape survivors in accessing justice, including victim-blaming, social stigma, and systemic barriers within the legal system. Through a critical analysis of the legal framework, the book highlights the gaps and weaknesses in the legal system and provides recommendations for legal reforms to ensure justice for rape survivors. The book also emphasizes the need for broader social and cultural changes to address the root causes of sexual violence, including gender inequality and patriarchal attitudes. Through a combination of legal analysis and advocacy, the book provides a valuable resource for scholars, legal professionals, policymakers, and activists working towards ending sexual violence and promoting gender justice in India[23].

Mukherjee, S. (2016). he article examines the historical and cultural factors that contribute to sexual violence in India and the various legal and policy responses to the problem. It also explores the challenges and barriers faced by rape survivors in accessing justice, including the lack of trust in the criminal justice system, victim- blaming, and social stigma. Through a critical analysis of the legal framework, the article highlights the gaps and weaknesses in the legal system and provides recommendations for legal reforms to ensure justice for rape survivors. The article also emphasizes the need for broader social and cultural changes to address the root causes of sexual violence, including gender inequality and patriarchal attitudes. Through a combination of legal analysis and advocacy, the article provides a valuable resource for scholars, legal professionals, policymakers, and activists working towards ending sexual violence and promoting gender justice in India. The article concludes with a call to action for legal professionals, policymakers, and civil society to work together to improve the legal framework and ensure that rape survivors receive justice and support. Overall, the article provides a comprehensive and critical analysis of the legal landscape of rape in India and the need for legal and social reforms to address this critical issue[24].

- **Criminal Law (Amendment) Act, 2013 (The Anti-Rape Act)**

The Criminal Law (Amendment) Act, 2013, commonly known as the Anti-Rape Act, is a significant legal reform aimed at addressing the pervasive problem of sexual violence in India. The Act was passed in response to the brutal gang rape and murder of a young woman on a bus in Delhi in December 2012, which sparked nationwide protests and calls for stronger legal protections for women.

The Anti-Rape Act introduced several important changes to the legal framework relating to sexual violence in India, including:

Expanded definition of rape: The Act expanded the definition of rape to include acts such as penetration by any object, and made it gender-neutral, recognizing that men can also be victims of rape.

Stricter punishment for rape: The Act increased the minimum punishment for rape from seven to ten years, and introduced the possibility of life imprisonment or the death penalty in cases of rape resulting in the victim's death or permanent vegetative state.

Criminalization of acid attacks: The Act criminalized acid attacks, imposing a minimum punishment of ten years and a maximum punishment of life imprisonment for such offenses.

New offenses: The Act introduced new offenses such as stalking and voyeurism, and imposed stringent punishments for these offenses.

Protection for victims and witnesses: The Act provided for the protection of victims and witnesses, including measures such as in-camera trials, anonymity for victims, and witness protection programs.

Changes in the legal process: The Act introduced several changes in the legal process relating to sexual violence cases, including the mandatory registration of First Information Reports (FIRs) in cases of rape, the establishment of fast-track courts for rape cases, and the prohibition of cross-examination of victims' sexual history in rape trials.

The Anti-Rape Act was a significant legal reform that aimed to address the pervasive problem of sexual violence in India. However, the implementation of the Act has been subject to several challenges, including:

Weak enforcement: Despite the stringent punishments introduced by the Act, there have been concerns about weak enforcement and low conviction rates in rape cases.

Social attitudes: There continue to be deep-rooted social attitudes and beliefs that perpetuate the problem of sexual violence in India, including victim-blaming and stigmatization of rape victims.

Lack of resources: There is a lack of resources and support for victims of sexual violence in India, including inadequate victim support services and limited access to legal aid.

Bureaucratic hurdles: There are bureaucratic hurdles involved in accessing compensation and support for victims of sexual violence, including complex application procedures and delays in processing claims.

To address these challenges, there is a need for greater resources and support for victims of sexual violence, including dedicated victim support services and legal aid. There is also a need for greater awareness and education about sexual violence and its impact on victims and society as a whole. Additionally, there is a need for stronger enforcement mechanisms and greater accountability for perpetrators of sexual violence, as well as better coordination and collaboration among stakeholders involved in addressing sexual violence.

The Anti-Rape Act was an important legal reform aimed at addressing the pervasive problem of sexual violence in India. While the implementation of the Act has been subject to several challenges, there is a need to continue to build on the legal framework established by the Act and to address the challenges faced by victims of sexual violence in India. By working together to address these challenges, India can move closer towards a society where women are free from the threat of sexual violence and are able to exercise their rights and freedoms without fear.

III

Compensation for Rape Victims

· Introduction

A person commits an illegal act when the benefits outweigh the costs, in this case the penalties they face for doing so. There are always three victims in a criminal act: society, the primary victim, and the victim's dependent. In the same way that the state uses laws like the Penal Code (1860) and the Code of Criminal Procedure (1973) to punish criminals, so does society. The actual victim, however, who has lost something because of the crime, has very little say in the prosecution and is instead at the mercy of investigators and public prosecutors. By punishing the perpetrators and sending a message that criminal behaviour will not be tolerated, society satisfies its thirst for vengeance, and victims receive what is commonly known as justice. This piece will focus on the crime of rape and the need for victims to receive restitution through a fair trial that affords them prompt justice and adequate protections.

The criminal law of any nation serves both as a deterrent to criminal behaviour and as a means of punishing those who commit crimes against the public. Different types of wrongdoing carry different penalties, and these are all addressed in the criminal law. Violence against women, including rape, falls under this category in India. Rape is defined in Section 375 of the Indian Penal Code, 1970, and its punishment is discussed in Section 376. In Shri Bodhisattwa Gautam v. Miss Subhra Chakraborty, the Supreme Court made the remarkable observation that compensation for rape victims is an essential part of the 'right to life[25].

> *"Rape is not only a crime against the person of a woman (victim), it is a crime against the entire society. It destroys the entire psychology of a woman and pushed her into deep emotional crises. It is only by her sheer will power that she rehabilitates herself in the society which, on coming to know of the rape, looks down upon her in derision and contempt. Rape is, therefore, the most hated crime. It is a crime against basic human rights and is also violative of the victim's most cherished of the Fundamental Rights, namely, the Right to Life contained in Article 21."*

In a society where the victim of rape is treated worse than the perpetrator, it is undeniable that financial compensation to the victim is crucial to her recovery. This aids the victim not only monetarily, but also in her efforts to lead a normal life.

- **Why is victim compensation important?**

Criminology (the study of criminal behaviour), Penology (the study of punishments for criminal acts), and Victimology (the study of victims of criminal behaviour) are the three main branches of study that make up the Criminal Justice System (a comparatively newer branch which centres around the measures such as compensation, rehabilitation, and justice to the victim). The criminal justice process has evolved from private vengeance to state-administered justice, with little consideration given to the victim. In the 1950s, British Magistrate and social reformer Margery Fry was among the first to advocate for modern victim compensation programs. In 1985, the United Nations unanimously adopted the Declaration of Basic Principles of Justice for Victims of Crime and Abuse of Power, which includes Clause 8, addressing victim compensation.

The Indian Constitution mandates, in Articles 41 and 51-A, that the government provide "the right to public assistance in cases of disability and in other cases of undeserved want," as well as "have compassion for living creatures" and "develop humanism." In Maru Ram v. Union of India, Justice Krishna Iyer argued that the growing field of victimology within humane criminal justice must find its fulfilment not through barbarity but through the wrongdoer's obligatory recoupment of the damage inflicted, not by causing the wrongdoer more suffering but by alleviating the victim's loss[26].

In 2003, the Justice Malimath Committee declared that victims of crime play a crucial role in criminal justice administration, serving as complainants, informants, and witnesses for the police and prosecution. Despite their vital role, criminal justice systems have traditionally prioritized the offender and his interests, often neglecting or completely disregarding those of the victim. Historically, civil law systems have placed greater value on victims compared to criminal justice systems. In Ankush Shivaji Gaikwad v. State of Maharashtra, it was declared that the objective of the provision is to allow the Court to direct the State to pay compensation to victims if the compensation awarded under Section 357 is inadequate, or if the case ends in acquittal or discharge and the victim needs rehabilitation. If the accused is not prosecuted, but the victim still requires rehabilitation, they may file a claim for financial compensation with the State or District Legal Services Authority.

- **Victim compensation regime**

Section 545 of the Criminal Procedure Code of 1898 provides for the payment of compensation to the injured party, as noted by the Law Commission of India. It is unfortunate that our courts do not use the broad discretion granted to them by this statute. There's no denying that there are constraints on what can be said in this paragraph. It will only be used if the court agrees that a hefty fine is an appropriate penalty for the offence at hand. If the victim of the crime has been ignored by the public prosecutor and no effort has been made to secure compensation for him, the court may decide that even the harshest penalties, including a lengthy prison sentence, are too lenient. The Supreme Court later noted the lower courts' callousness in Hari Singh v. Sukhbir Singh and, while ordering them to use their authority liberally, noted that despite Section 357's importance, it is rarely invoked by lower courts, possibly because of a lack of understanding of the provision's purpose[27].

After much back-and-forth, Section 357-A CrPC was added to the Criminal Procedure Code to empower the State to establish a Victim Compensation Scheme. The victim shall be compensated in accordance with such scheme, taking into account the specifics of the incident. The State Legal Services Authority or the District Legal Services Authority must investigate. Current provisions of law, such as Sections 357, 357-A, 357-B, 357-C, 358, and 359 of CrPC, address victim compensation. In addition, the complainant is liable for compensation under Section 250 CrPC, 1973, if the prosecution was initiated based on a false accusation and the person was ultimately acquitted after trial and the trial court found that a false case was foisted. The accused is the one wrongly targeted in such cases. The accused in a criminal case may also experience hardship due to the wrongful actions of the complainant or the state. Even filing a false First Information Report (FIR) can lead to social stigma. As a result, if an accusation is made without reasonable cause and the court determines that a false case was filed, the court may order compensation under Section 250 CrPC for the accused.

The recommendations of the Law Commission of India resulted in the consolidation of Sections 545 and 546 of the former Code of Criminal Procedure, 1898 into what is now Section 357 of the CrPC. In Palaniappa Gounder v. State of T.N., the Supreme Court made the observation that an order for compensa The Law Commission of India's recommendations resulted in the consolidation of former Code of Criminal Procedure, 1898 Sections 545 and 546 into what is now Section 357 of the CrPC. In Palaniappa Gounder v. State of T.N., the Supreme Court clarified that compensation under Section 357(1)(c) can only be awarded when the court imposes a fine or a sentence that includes a fine. Sections 357-A and 357-B expanded the scope of the victim compensation system. Prior to this amendment, it was solely the responsibility of the accused to compensate the victim following the trial, but the State had no such obligation. compensation under Section 357(1)(c) can only be made when a Court imposes a sentence of fine or a sentence of which fine forms a part. The scope of the victim compensation system was expanded with the inclusion of Sections 357-A and 357-B. It was the responsibility of the accused to compensate the victim following the conclusion of the trial, but the State had no such responsibility prior to this amendment. Since the victim compensation scheme is retroactive, victims who are due compensation for crimes committed before the scheme went into effect will not be denied that compensation. If a victim's right to life is violated, then denying or delaying compensation would "continue such violation and perpetrate gross inhumanity on the victim in question," as stated in Section 357-A."

In the case of Ashwani Gupta v. Govt. of India, the Delhi High Court ruled that punishing the offender alone would not console the victim's family. Section 357 compensation was deemed more practical and efficient than a civil action for damages due to the latter's lengthy and complex nature. Krishna Iyer J. in Rattan Singh v. State of Punjab identified the neglect of crime victims by the legal system as a flaw. In many jurisdictions, particularly in Europe, victims of crime have two types of rights: (1) the right to participate in criminal proceedings, and (2) the right to seek and receive compensation from the criminal court for injuries resulting from the crime.

In Karan v. State NCT of Delhi, decided by a three-judge bench of the Delhi High Court, the Court reaffirmed its obligation to consider the issue of victim compensation under Section 357 of the CrPC in every criminal case[28]. In every criminal case, the court must explain why it awarded or denied compensation, as this is an exercise of discretion on the part of the judge. The court laid out the following procedures, while noting that the amount of compensation is ultimately up to the courts to decide based on factors like the seriousness of the offence, the extent of the victim's mental and physical harm/injury, the extent of any property damage or losses, and the accused's ability to pay[29]:

1. Within 10 days of the defendant's conviction, the trial court must order him to file an affidavit with the court detailing his assets and income, along with supporting documentation. Within 30 days of the conviction, the State must file an affidavit detailing the costs associated with the prosecution.

2. If the accused cannot pay the compensation or if the compensation awarded against the accused is insufficient for the victim's rehabilitation, then the court shall recommend the case to the Delhi State Legal Services Authority for award of compensation from the victim compensation fund under the Delhi, Victims Compensation Scheme, 2018.

3. During the trial, the court must consider the victim impact report and hear from all parties involved, including the victim(s). If the accused has the financial means, the court may order compensation to be paid to the victim(s) and cover the cost of the prosecution for the State. The accused must deposit the compensation with DSLSA, and DSLSA will distribute the funds to the victims according to their own scheme, as directed by

the court.

4. The trial court, upon receiving the accused's affidavit, shall forward to the Delhi State Legal Services Authority a copy of the judgement and the affidavit (DSLSA). The DSLSA will then conduct a brief investigation to assess the victim's loss and the defendant's ability to pay. Within 30 days, it must submit the victim impact report along with its suggestions. For this purpose, the DSLSA may contact the relevant SDM, SHO, and/or prosecution for advice and/or assistance.

5. The public prosecutor shall file an application pursuant to Section 357(4) of the CrPC seeking the court's direction for enforcing this procedure in matters of appeal or revision where Section 357 has not been complied with.

- **Compensation for offences against women**

Rape is widely considered one of the most atrocious crimes committed against humanity, as it entails not only the transaction cost but also the social and psychological costs. In the case of Bodhisattwa Gautam v. Subhra Chakraborty, the Supreme Court emphasized that rape is not just an offense against an individual woman, but a crime that harms society as a whole. It destroys a woman's mental and emotional well-being, leaving her in a state of deep trauma and psychological distress. It is only through her sheer willpower that she can recover and reintegrate into society, which often views her with disdain and contempt after learning of the rape. Rape is widely regarded as the most abhorrent crime, violating fundamental human rights and infringing on the victim's most fundamental right to life, as enshrined in Article 21.[30].

The Nirbhaya Fund was established after the Criminal Law (Amendment) Act, 2013 was passed to fill the gap in protections for victims of sexual crimes against women and children. By notification dated 14 October 2015 from the Ministry of Home Affairs, the Central Government also established the Central Victim Compensation Fund Scheme. However, only 36% of the Nirbhaya Fund had been used in the past seven years, according to a report from last year, which speaks volumes about the enforcement backdrops apropos India's bureaucracy. Additionally, 98% of the minor rape victims who experienced sexual assault had not received any form of financial compensation. The Supreme Court of India, in the case of Nipun Saxena v. Union of India, instructed the National Legal Services Authority (NALSA) to establish a Committee to develop Model Rules for Victim Compensation in cases of Sexual Offenses and Acid Attacks. The Committee subsequently formulated the 2018 Compensation Scheme for Women Victims/Survivors of Sexual Assault and other Crimes. According to the program, a victim of gang rape is eligible for compensation ranging from Rs 5 lakhs to Rs 10 lakhs, while a victim of rape or severe sexual assault may receive between Rs 4 lakhs and Rs 7 lakhs in compensation. The victims of acid attacks would receive a minimum of Rs 7 lakhs and a maximum of Rs 8 lakhs in compensation for facial disfigurement. After that, the court ruled that the nationwide scheme in question would indeed be upheld as valid and thus would continue to be legally binding throughout India.

- **A Brief Analysis Of Different Victim Compensation Schemes**

After the 2008 amendment, almost every state in India introduced its own victim compensation program. These programs, in accordance with Section 357A, seek to provide compensation to victims or their dependents who have suffered harm or loss due to the crime and require rehabilitation. While most state programs provide financial compensation, the victim compensation schemes in Odisha and Meghalaya go beyond monetary aid and also offer tailored services such as shelter, counselling, medical assistance, legal aid, education, and vocational training to meet the specific needs of the victim. This is a huge improvement for rape victims, whose lives may have been completely derailed after the traumatic event. The victim can get a fresh start with the help of the state's educational and vocational programmes and other available services. For the same reason, other states' victim compensation programmes should incorporate something similar into their programmes[31].

If we look at the definition clause for the term 'victim' in the Assam Victim Compensation Scheme, 2012, it defines victim as:

> *"Victim means a person who has suffered any loss or injury caused by the reason of the act or omission for which the accused person has been charged"*

The term "has been charged" refers to a suspect who has been identified, investigated, and formally charged by the court in accordance with the Criminal Procedure Code. However, this definition contradicts the law as stated in Section 357A of the Criminal Procedure Code, which allows victims to seek compensation under the compensation scheme even if the offender has not been identified.

Moreover, this definition appears to go against the objectives of the victim compensation programs in Himachal Pradesh and Assam.

The lack of a governing body or authority is another issue with most of these victim compensation schemes. When considering this issue, other states may look to Madhya Pradesh's Victim Compensation Scheme as a model. Provision has been made for the scheme to be monitored under the Madhya Pradesh Victim Compensation Scheme. Each state will have to set up a Victim Compensation Scheme Committee and a District Victim Compensation Scheme Committee to keep an eye on things. It is crucial to have a centralised body responsible for overseeing the Victim Compensation Scheme in order to evaluate how well the programmes are working. It makes sure that if the scheme doesn't work as intended, the government and policy implementers will be held responsible.

Many victim compensation programmes do not specify the reasons an application for compensation would be denied. Most of these programmes also do not require the State or District Legal Services Authority to explain why they did not grant the victim/applicant the requested compensation. If compensation is denied, however, the authority must provide a reasoned order under the Delhi Victim Compensation Scheme, 2015, detailing the reasons for the denial.

The victim compensation schemes in the states of Himachal Pradesh, Madhya Pradesh, Goa, and Karnataka all specify grounds for rejecting, withholding, or reducing compensation. Here are a few of the points everyone can agree on:

- Furnishing false evidence
- Failure to report the crime
- Failure to co-operate with police/authority
- Failure to give reasonable assistance to DLSA/SLSA
- Facts and Circumstances of the victim make his/her ineligible for compensation, etc.

Most of the reasons given for denying an application seem reasonable, but it would be unfair to deny those who have been the victims of serious crimes like rape because they did not provide reasonable assistance to the authorities. Due to the ongoing emotional and psychological distress, a rape victim may be unable to provide her full cooperation.

These state victim compensation schemes do not adhere to any sort of standardisation. Eligibility requirements and limitations vary from one state to the next. For example, only BPL families can apply for compensation through the Mizoram Victims of Crime Compensation Scheme.

Initially, there were significant disparities between the Victim Compensation Schemes offered by different states. In the case of Tekan Alias Tekram v. the State of M.P, the Supreme Court observed that the amount of compensation provided by each state under their respective schemes for rape cases varied considerably. To address this, the Court conducted a review of the compensation amounts awarded by each state to rape victims. The Court brought attention to this disparity by noting that victims of rape in Jharkhand were only eligible to receive a maximum of Rs. 20,000 in compensation under the state's victim compensation scheme, while victims of rape in Goa were eligible to receive a maximum of Rs. 10 lakhs under the state's victim compensation scheme[32].

This disparity in payments prompted the government to draught the Central Victim Compensation Fund Scheme Guidelines in 2015. This project received Rs. 200 cr from the Nirbhaya Fund. All State Victim Compensation Schemes have been brought into conformity with the Central Scheme's minimum compensation of Rs. 3 lakhs for rape. Even though the guidelines were issued in 2015, many states have not updated their victim compensation systems to reflect the new standards.

· Central Victim Compensation Scheme

The Honorable Supreme Court of India requested that NALSA form a committee in 2012 to draught Model Rules for Victim Compensation for sexual offences and acid attacks, following the case Nipun Saxena Vs. Union of India. Accordingly, in 2018, the Supreme Court approved NALSA's "Compensation Scheme for Women Victims/Survivors of Sexual Assault/other Crime." This is a historic step because it established the framework for a new component of a state compensation scheme that is tailored to victims of sexual assault and acid attacks. The scheme specifies both a minimum and maximum amount of compensation that can be awarded for the specified offences[33].

It requires law enforcement to notify the SLSA/DSLA of any crimes committed that fall under the purview of this programme by providing both paper and electronic copies of the police report. The law grants SLSA/DLSA the power to conduct preliminary fact- finding on their own initiative, without a formal request. In certain circumstances, immediate compensation ranging from Rs. 5,000 to 10,000 may be granted. As per the Central Victim Compensation Fund Scheme Guidelines, the minimum compensation amount for rape cases has been raised, with a minimum of Rs. 4 lakhs awarded in cases of rape and a minimum of Rs. 5 lakhs granted in cases of gang rape.

The programme marks a major step forward in the empowerment and recovery of victimised women. The scheme's implementation was relatively recent, however, so we have not yet had a chance to evaluate its results.

- **Global Scenarios**

A. Scenario in UK:

The Criminal Injuries Compensation Authority was established in 1964 and is charged with overseeing the Criminal Injuries Compensation Scheme for the whole of England, Wales, and Scotland.

The compensation for each injury has been set at a fixed amount between 1,000 and 250,000 British pounds since 1996. In addition, applicants can receive up to UK $250,000 in compensation for lost wages and extraordinary costs.

Previously supported by the Home Office, the scheme is now fully funded by the Ministry of Justice. For both nonfatal and fatal injuries, victims and their dependents are legally entitled to monetary compensation. Medical costs, funeral costs, lost wages, mental stress and trauma, special care medical costs, and reputational harm are all compensable.

The applicant's criminal history, relevant police reports, and medical records are just some of the factors the Authority considers when making compensation decisions. When the Authority makes a ruling, there is an appeals process available.

B. Scenario in Canada:

Numerous Canadian provinces have implemented laws to guarantee compensation for victims of crimes. For instance, the Ontario Compensation for Victims of Crime Act, 1990 enables the establishment of a Criminal Injuries Compensation Board. This legislation allows victims, their dependents, or their caretakers to claim compensation.

Compensation may cover various costs that are reasonably and actually incurred due to the victim's injury or death. This includes financial losses incurred by the victim due to total or partial disability affecting their ability to work, as well as financial losses incurred by dependents due to the victim's death. Compensation may also cover pain and suffering, support for a child born as a result of rape, and other financial losses resulting from the victim's injury. The Board may consider any expense that is deemed reasonable to be covered under compensation.

Furthermore, the Board is authorised to grant compensation in place of any common law rights that the victim may have. It is worth noting that compensation can be granted regardless of whether the offender has been convicted, indicating a shift from a punitive approach to a restorative one. Compensation can be provided in a single lump sum payment, in instalments, or as directed by the Board.

C. Scenario in USA and Australia:

Similar compensation programs exist in the United States and Australia, with many states and territories enacting legislation and budget allocations to guarantee compensation for victims of crimes.

The Criminal Injuries Compensation Act 2003 in Western Australia provides victims with the option to seek compensation for incidents reported to the police, regardless of whether a perpetrator has been identified, charged, or convicted. Compensation can be awarded for various types of harm resulting from an offence, such as bodily harm, mental or nervous shock, or pregnancy. The compensation can cover expenses such as pain and suffering, loss of enjoyment of life, loss of income, medical expenses, and other incidental expenses, such as travel for medical purposes.

- **Treatment or damage of clothing:**

A. Indian Scenario, Compensation and the Constitution

Rape is a violation of fundamental rights guaranteed under Article 21 of the Indian Constitution. To compensate for this violation, the State may be penalized for breaching its public law duty and violating fundamental rights. This compensation is known as 'exemplary damages' and is awarded against the wrongdoer for breaching public law duty, in addition to any compensation granted under the law of torts for loss or injury.[34].

Justice Krishna Ayyar, in 1980, pointed out the weakness in the Indian legal system that fails to focus on the victims of the crime and the distress of the prisoner's dependents. He urged the Legislature to rectify this deficiency and draw attention to the matter of victim reparation, which is still the vanishing point of the criminal law in India. [Source: "Rattan Singh vs. State of Punjab" AIR 1980 Supreme Court 84]

Modern victimology recognizes that crime victims have the right to adequate compensation, rehabilitation, and restoration, regardless of whether the offender is identified and prosecuted. The state is responsible for paying such compensation.[35].

B. Compensatory Justice:

The focus of criminal justice has expanded beyond the traditional goals of retribution and deterrence. There is now a greater emphasis on compensating victims through a more victim-centered approach. Several societies have developed methods to address these concerns.

Compensatory justice is not only about rehabilitating the victim, but also about creating a societal framework that recognizes the severity of such crimes and provides some form of compensation to the victim.

Many countries around the world have been implementing the concept of a publicly funded and administered body to compensate victims of violent crime for some time now. Compensation is not only granted when the State is at fault but also when the crime is violent and serious, and thus the role of the State takes on a welfare dimension.

C. Scheme drafted by the NCW:

The National Commission for Women in India created the Scheme for the Rehabilitation for Victims of Rape, 2005 following the Supreme Court's directive in the Delhi Domestic Working Women's Forum case.

The Scheme for the Rehabilitation for Victims of Rape, 2005 in India proposed the establishment of Criminal Injuries and Rehabilitation Boards at the District and State levels, as well as a National Criminal Injuries and Rehabilitation Board.

The scheme gives details about the constitution, functions and the budgetary allocation of the Authorities constituted under it.

The scheme offers compensation to victims of rape, regardless of whether the offender has been prosecuted or not. It also includes provisions for legal aid and other forms of assistance to help victims. However, there is no indication of any additional consideration on these matters, or the government's willingness to take them further.

In the Bodhtswa case of 1996, the Supreme Court recognised the victim's right to compensation and referred to the previous judgment of the Delhi Domestic Working Women's Forum case of 1994. The court held that compensation should be awarded to the victim by the court upon conviction of the offender, subject to the finalisation of a scheme by the Central Government. The court also observed that if the court has jurisdiction to award compensation at the final stage, then there is no reason to deny the right to award interim compensation, which should also be provided for in the scheme.

In line with the Delhi Domestic Working Women's Forum decision, courts trying rape cases have the jurisdiction to award interim compensation as part of their overall jurisdiction, given that rape is an offence against basic human rights.

- **Justifications for Compensation:** Various justifications for compensation have been used, such as:

1. Benefit to the victims,
2. Symbolic social recognition for the victim's suffering,

Deterrent effects on the offender as also the reformative effects on the offender as the paying of compensation has an "intrinsic moral value of its own".

- **Evolution of Victim Compensation Fund:**

After the 9/11 terrorist attacks in the United States, the Victim Compensation Fund (VCF) was established to provide monetary aid to the victims and their families who suffered injuries or lost their lives in the attacks.

The Victim Compensation Fund (VCF) was established to provide financial aid to the victims and their families following the September 11, 2001 terrorist attacks in the United States. The original VCF operated from 2001 to 2004, granting over $7 billion in compensation. However, the program faced criticism for delays and bureaucratic obstacles.

In 2010, the James Zadroga 9/11 Health and Compensation Act was passed, reopening the VCF and extending compensation to those affected by the attacks until 2020. The program was expanded to cover additional health conditions related to the attacks. In 2015, the VCF faced a funding shortfall due to a rise in claims and payouts for cancer- related illnesses. The James Zadroga 9/11 Health and Compensation Reauthorization Act was passed, providing an extra $4.6 billion in funding and extending the program through 2020.

President Trump signed the Never Forget the Heroes: James Zadroga, Ray Pfeifer, and Luis Alvarez Permanent Authorization of the September 11th Victim Compensation Fund Act in July 2019. The Act made the VCF permanent and allocated additional funds to ensure that all eligible claims could be paid.

The VCF still operates today and offers compensation to people impacted by the 9/11 attacks, such as first responders, residents, and lower Manhattan workers during the aftermath. The program has distributed more than $11 billion in compensation so far, making it one of the most significant victim compensation programs in the history of the United States.

- **International Aspect**

While the Victim Compensation Fund is specific to the United States and its response to the September 11 attacks, there are similar programs in other countries that provide compensation to victims of terrorism and other violent crimes.

In Europe, the European Union has established a framework for victim compensation that includes minimum standards for victim compensation and assistance across EU member states. Each member state is responsible for implementing and enforcing the framework within their own jurisdiction.

The United Nations has also recognized the importance of victim compensation and has called on member states to provide assistance and support to victims of terrorism, including compensation for their losses. The UN has established a Counter-Terrorism Committee Executive Directorate (CTED) to assist member states in implementing these measures.

Many countries also have programs that provide compensation to victims of violent crimes, such as the Crime Victims Compensation Program in the United States and the Criminal Injuries Compensation Scheme in the United Kingdom.

Overall, victim compensation programs are an important aspect of supporting victims of terrorism and other violent crimes, and can help to provide financial support and assistance to those who have suffered as a result of these tragic events.

- **Fundamental Principles for Ensuring Justice for Victims of Crime and Abuse of Power**

The principles of justice for victims of crime and abuse of power are fundamental guidelines that aim to provide fair and equitable treatment to individuals who have suffered harm as a result of criminal acts or abuse of power.

These principles are based on the belief that victims of crime should have access to justice and support, and that their rights and interests should be taken into account throughout the criminal justice process. Key principles include providing victims with information about their rights and the criminal justice process, ensuring their safety and protection, and providing them with access to legal and other support services.

Other important principles include ensuring that victims are treated with dignity and respect, and that their views and needs are taken into account when decisions are made about their case. This includes giving victims the opportunity to participate in court proceedings and to provide input on decisions related to sentencing and other outcomes.

Overall, the principles of justice for victims of crime and abuse of power are essential for promoting fairness, equality, and accountability within the criminal justice system, and for ensuring that victims are given the support and assistance they need to recover from the harm they have experienced.

ॐ

IV

Case Law & Law Relating To Rape Victims In India

- **Case Law**

Here are significant case laws related to rape victims in India:

- **Tukaram v. State of Maharashtra (1979):** In Tukaram v. State of Maharashtra (1979), the Supreme Court of India established the principle that the testimony of a rape victim can be relied upon to convict the accused, even in the absence of any corroborating evidence. The court held that the testimony of a victim of sexual assault, if found to be truthful, is sufficient to establish the guilt of the accused beyond a reasonable doubt, and there is no requirement of corroboration in rape cases. The court emphasized that the evidentiary rule requiring corroboration in rape cases is a relic of the past and should be discarded. This case was a significant milestone in the development of the legal framework for protecting the rights of rape victims in India and has helped to ensure that victims' testimonies are given due weightage in court proceedings.

- **State of Punjab v. Gurmit Singh (1996):** In State of Punjab v. Gurmit Singh (1996), the Supreme Court of India held that a woman's evidence should be accepted in sexual assault cases, even if she is of "loose character." The court rejected the argument that a woman of "easy virtue" or "loose moral character" is more likely to make a false allegation of rape and held that such an argument is based on deep-rooted stereotypes and prejudices against women. The court emphasized that the character of the victim is irrelevant in a rape case and that the focus should be on the accused's conduct. This case was significant in establishing that a woman's past sexual history or conduct cannot be used to undermine her credibility as a witness in a rape case and that rape victims should be treated with dignity and respect, regardless of their social status or background.

- **State of Haryana v. Bhajan Lal (1992):** In State of Haryana v. Bhajan Lal (1992), the Supreme Court of India recognized that sexual harassment of women is a violation of their fundamental rights and can be redressed under Article 32 of the Indian Constitution. The court held that sexual harassment, whether at the workplace or elsewhere, is a form of violence against women and can result in physical, psychological, and economic harm. The court also observed that the existing laws and procedures for redressing sexual harassment were inadequate and that women faced significant barriers in accessing justice. The court directed the government to implement guidelines to prevent and redress sexual harassment, including the appointment of Complaints Committees to receive and investigate complaints of sexual harassment. This case was significant in recognizing sexual harassment as a violation of women's rights and in establishing the legal framework for addressing and preventing sexual harassment in India.

- **Bodhisattwa Gautam v. Subhra Chakraborty (1996):** In Bodhisattwa Gautam v. Subhra Chakraborty (1996), the Supreme Court of India recognized the right of rape victims to anonymity and privacy and directed courts to use pseudonyms instead of the victim's real name in court proceedings. The court held that rape victims face significant stigma and social ostracism, and revealing their identity can result in further harm and trauma. The court also observed that the use of pseudonyms can protect the victim's right to privacy and dignity and can encourage other victims to come forward and report sexual violence. This case was significant in establishing the principle of victim anonymity in rape cases in India and in ensuring that rape victims are treated with sensitivity and respect by the legal system.

- **State of Karnataka v. Krishnappa (2000):** In State of Karnataka v. Krishnappa (2000), the Supreme Court of India held that the victim's prior sexual history or conduct is not relevant in a rape case. The court observed that a victim's past sexual history or conduct is not indicative of her consent in the current case and can only be used to undermine her credibility and reputation. The court emphasized that the victim's character or conduct is not relevant to the question of whether rape occurred or not and that the focus should be on the accused's conduct. This case was significant in establishing that a victim's past sexual history or conduct cannot be used to justify or excuse rape and that the accused's conduct should be the sole basis for determining guilt or innocence in a rape case.

- **State of Rajasthan v. N.K. (2000):** In State of Rajasthan v. N.K. (2000), the Supreme Court of India held that rape victims are entitled to compensation under the Victim Compensation Scheme, and the quantum of compensation should be decided on a case-by-case basis. The court observed that rape victims suffer physical, psychological, and emotional harm as a result of the crime, and compensation can help to alleviate some of their suffering and provide them with a sense of justice. The court also observed that the state has a duty to protect the rights of victims and ensure that they receive adequate compensation and support. This case was significant in recognizing the importance of compensation for rape victims in India and in establishing the legal framework for providing such compensation.

- **State of Himachal Pradesh v. Asha Ram (2005):** In State of Himachal Pradesh v. Asha Ram (2005), the Supreme Court of India held that medical evidence is not necessary to prove rape if the victim's testimony is credible and reliable. The court observed that rape is a crime that often occurs in private and that there may not be any medical evidence to corroborate the victim's testimony. The court held that in such cases, the victim's testimony should be given the highest weightage and that minor discrepancies in her testimony do not reduce its evidentiary value. The court also observed that medical evidence can be used to support the victim's testimony but cannot be a substitute for it. This case was significant in establishing that a victim's testimony alone can be sufficient to establish the guilt of the accused in a rape case and that the absence of medical evidence does not necessarily undermine the credibility of the victim's testimony.

- **State of Uttar Pradesh v. Chhotey Lal (2008):** In State of Uttar Pradesh v. Chhotey Lal (2008), the Supreme Court of India held that the absence of injuries on the victim's body does not mean that rape did not occur. The court observed that the absence of injuries does not necessarily mean that the victim did not resist or that the accused did not use force or coercion to commit the crime. The court held that the victim's testimony, if found credible and reliable, can be sufficient to establish the guilt of the accused, even in the absence of injuries or medical evidence. The court emphasized that rape victims often face significant trauma and may not be able to resist or fight back, and that the absence of injuries should not be used to question the veracity of their testimony. This case was significant in recognizing that the absence of injuries on the victim's body does not necessarily undermine the credibility of her testimony and in ensuring that rape victims are not subjected to further trauma or victim-blaming based on physical evidence.

- **Bhanwari Devi v. State of Rajasthan (1995):** In Bhanwari Devi v. State of Rajasthan (1995), the Supreme Court of India held that sexual harassment at the workplace is a violation of women's rights, and employers have a duty to provide a safe and harassment-free workplace. The case involved the sexual assault of a lower-caste woman, Bhanwari Devi, by upper-caste men who were angered by her attempts to prevent child marriage. The court observed that sexual harassment at the workplace is a form of violence against women and can result in physical, psychological, and economic harm. The court held that employers have a duty to prevent and redress sexual harassment and that they should implement measures such as Complaints Committees, awareness programs, and training for employees to prevent sexual harassment at the workplace. This case was significant in recognizing sexual harassment as a violation of women's rights and in establishing the legal framework for addressing and preventing sexual harassment in the workplace in India.

- **State of Maharashtra v. Madhukar Narayan Mardikar (1991)** In State of Maharashtra v. Madhukar Narayan Mardikar (1991), the Supreme Court of India held that the victim's evidence in rape cases should be given the highest weightage and that minor discrepancies in her testimony do not reduce its evidentiary value. The court observed that rape is a traumatic experience for the victim and that she may not be able to recall every detail of the incident or may make minor errors in her testimony. The court held that such minor discrepancies should not be used to undermine the victim's credibility and that her testimony should be evaluated as a whole. The court also observed that the victim's evidence should be given the highest weightage, as she is the best judge of her experience. This case was significant in establishing that the victim's testimony should be given the highest weightage in a rape case and that minor discrepancies or errors should not be used to question the veracity of her testimony.

- **Lalita Kumari v. Government of Uttar Pradesh (2013):** In Lalita Kumari v. Government of Uttar Pradesh (2013), the Supreme Court of India held that the police have a duty to register a First Information Report (FIR) in all cases of rape and sexual assault, and failure to do so can result in disciplinary action against the concerned officers. The court observed that the failure to register an FIR can result in a denial of justice for the victim and can also lead to the accused going unpunished. The court held that the police should not conduct a preliminary inquiry or verification before registering an FIR in a case of rape or sexual assault, and that they should register the FIR immediately upon receipt of the complaint. The court also directed the government to issue guidelines to ensure the effective implementation of this ruling. This case was significant in ensuring that the police take prompt action in cases of rape and sexual assault and in establishing a legal framework to ensure that victims receive timely and effective justice.
- **State of Punjab v. Ramdev Singh (2004):** In State of Punjab v. Ramdev Singh (2004), the Supreme Court of India held that the accused's past criminal record can be used to prove his character and behavior in a rape case. The court observed that a person's past conduct is indicative of his character and that evidence of his past criminal record can be used to establish his propensity to commit similar offenses. The court held that such evidence can be used to prove the accused's motive, intention, and modus operandi in committing the crime of rape. However, the court also observed that such

evidence should be relevant and material to the case and should not be used to prejudice the accused or to divert attention from the facts of the case. This case was significant in establishing that the accused's past criminal record can be used as evidence in a rape case and in ensuring that such evidence is used judiciously and fairly.

- **State of Rajasthan v. Om Prakash (2002):** In State of Rajasthan v. Om Prakash (2002), the Supreme Court of India held that a medical examination report is not conclusive evidence in a rape case and should be evaluated in conjunction with other evidence, including the victim's testimony. The case involved the rape of a minor girl, and the medical examination report did not provide conclusive evidence of rape. The court observed that medical examination reports are important pieces of evidence in a rape case, but they should not be given undue weightage. The court held that the victim's testimony should be evaluated along with the medical examination report, and if the victim's testimony is found to be credible and reliable, it can be sufficient to establish the guilt of the accused. The court also observed that the medical examination report should not be used to disbelieve the victim's testimony or to question her credibility. This case was significant in establishing that the medical examination report is not conclusive evidence in a rape case and that the victim's testimony should be given due weightage in evaluating the evidence.

- **State of Uttar Pradesh v. Man Singh (2010):** In State of Uttar Pradesh v. Man Singh (2010), the Supreme Court of India held that the burden of proof in a rape case rests solely on the prosecution, and the accused is presumed innocent until proven guilty beyond a reasonable doubt. The court observed that rape is a heinous crime, and the accused should not be convicted on the basis of conjectures, surmises, or probabilities. The court held that the prosecution must prove each and every element of the offense of rape beyond a reasonable doubt, and any doubts or ambiguities should be resolved in favor of the accused. The court also observed that the victim's testimony should be evaluated with care and caution, and if it is found to be unreliable or inconsistent, it should not be used to convict the accused. This case was significant in establishing the legal standard for proving the offense of rape in India and in ensuring that the accused's right to a fair trial is protected.

- **Delhi Domestic Working Women's Forum v. Union of India (1995):** In Delhi Domestic Working Women's Forum v. Union of India (1995), the Supreme Court of India recognized the right of domestic workers to be protected from sexual harassment and exploitation. The case involved the sexual exploitation of a domestic worker by her employer, and the court observed that domestic workers are often vulnerable to sexual exploitation due to their social and economic status. The court held that domestic workers have the right to a safe and harassment-free workplace, and employers have a duty to prevent and redress sexual harassment and exploitation. The court directed the government to implement measures such as Complaints Committees and awareness programs to prevent and redress sexual harassment of domestic workers. This case was significant in recognizing the rights of domestic workers in India and in establishing the legal framework for protecting them from sexual harassment and exploitation.

- **Vishakha v. State of Rajasthan (1997):** In Vishakha v. State of Rajasthan (1997), the Supreme Court of India recognized sexual harassment at the workplace as a violation of women's fundamental rights and established guidelines for preventing and redressing sexual harassment in the workplace. The case involved the gang rape of a social worker in a rural development program in Rajasthan. The court observed that sexual harassment at the workplace is a form of violence against women and can result in physical, psychological, and economic harm. The court held that employers have a duty to prevent and redress sexual harassment and that they should implement measures such as Complaints Committees, awareness programs, and training for employees to prevent sexual harassment at the workplace. The court also directed the government to issue guidelines to ensure the effective implementation of this ruling. This case was significant in recognizing sexual harassment as a violation of women's rights and in establishing the legal framework for addressing and preventing sexual harassment in the workplace in India.
- Law relating to rape victims in India

Here is a comprehensive list of laws and policies related to rape victims in India:

  - Indian Penal Code now Bhartiya Nyaya Sanhita (BNS)
  - Criminal Procedure Code now The Bharatiya Nagarik Suraksha Sanhita (BNSS)

- Protection of Children from Sexual Offences (POCSO) Act
- The Immoral Traffic (Prevention) Act, 195
- Sexual Harassment of Women at Workplace (Prevention, Prohibition, and Redressal) Act, 2013
- National Policy for Women
- Criminal Law (Amendment) Act, 2013 (The Anti-Rape Act)
- Medical Termination of Pregnancy (MTP) Act
- The Juvenile Justice (Care and Protection of Children) Act, 2015
- The Prohibition of Child Marriage Act, 2006
- The Domestic Violence Act, 2005
- The Mental Healthcare Act, 2017
- The Prevention of Atrocities Against Scheduled Castes and Scheduled Tribes Act, 1989
- The National Commission for Women Act, 1990
- The Rights of Persons with Disabilities Act, 2016
- The National Human Rights Commission Act, 1993
- The Information Technology (Amendment) Act, 2008
- The Representation of People Act, 1951
- The Dowry Prohibition Act, 1961
- The Equal Remuneration Act, 1976

These laws and policies aim to protect survivors of sexual violence, promote gender justice, and prevent the occurrence of sexual offenses. However, their implementation and effectiveness remain a challenge, and more work is needed to ensure that survivors receive justice and support.

Bhartiya Nyaya Sanhita: The Bharatiya Nyaya Sanhita (BNS) is the updated legal framework succeeding the Indian Penal Code (IPC) and aims to address the evolving needs of India's justice system, particularly concerning sexual offenses. The BNS retains and strengthens many of the provisions designed to protect victims of sexual violence, incorporating more stringent measures to ensure justice and support for survivors.

Despite these legal advancements, the implementation of the BNS faces significant challenges. Survivors often encounter systemic barriers such as societal stigma, procedural delays, and inadequate support services, which hinder their access to justice. The need for comprehensive legal and social reforms remains critical, focusing on addressing the root causes of sexual violence and fostering gender equality. This involves not only refining legal mechanisms but also promoting educational initiatives and societal change to create a more supportive environment for survivors and a more equitable society.

The Bharatiya Nagarik Suraksha Sanhita (BNSS): The Bharatiya Nagarik Suraksha Sanhita (BNSS), which has replaced the Criminal Procedure Code (CrPC), is a comprehensive procedural law that governs the investigation, trial, and punishment of criminal offenses in India. Its primary aim is to ensure that criminal trials are conducted in a fair, just, and transparent manner, safeguarding the rights of both the accused and the victim. The BNSS outlines the procedural framework for various stages of criminal proceedings, including the registration of complaints, the investigation process, the roles and responsibilities of the police and other authorities, the conduct of trials, and the sentencing of offenders. It encompasses all criminal cases, including those related to sexual offenses, and includes specific provisions to protect the privacy and dignity of victims. For instance, it mandates that a victim's statement can be recorded by a female police officer and ensures the protection of the victim's identity.

Additionally, the BNSS requires the mandatory registration of complaints related to sexual offenses and mandates that a police report be submitted to the magistrate for cognizable and non-bailable offenses, such as rape. Despite these provisions, the effective implementation of the BNSS remains a challenge. Survivors of sexual violence often face systemic barriers in accessing justice, including delays in the trial process, inadequate evidence collection, and a lack of sensitivity among the police and other authorities. Addressing these challenges is crucial to ensuring that the BNSS fulfills its purpose of providing justice and protection to victims of sexual violence.

Protection of Children from Sexual Offences (POCSO) Act. The Protection of Children from Sexual Offences (POCSO) Act is a legal framework that aims to protect children from sexual abuse and exploitation in India. The Act was enacted in 2012, and it provides a comprehensive framework for the prevention, protection, investigation, prosecution, and rehabilitation of children who are victims of sexual offenses.

The POCSO Act is an important legal framework for protecting children from sexual offenses in India. However, the implementation of the Act remains a challenge, and many survivors of sexual abuse continue to face barriers in accessing justice and support. There is a need for comprehensive legal and social reforms to address the root causes of sexual abuse and exploitation of children and to promote a safe and nurturing environment for children in

India.

Medical Termination of Pregnancy (MTP) Act The Medical Termination of Pregnancy (MTP) Act is a crucial legal framework that regulates the termination of pregnancy in India. The Act provides a legal and safe way for women to terminate unwanted pregnancies, thereby protecting their reproductive rights and promoting their health and well-being. Under the MTP Act, a pregnancy can be terminated up to 20 weeks if it poses a risk to the woman's physical or mental health, or if there is a risk of fetal abnormality. The procedure must be carried out by a registered medical practitioner in a hospital or clinic authorized to perform abortions, and the woman's consent is required. The Act also requires the maintenance of detailed records of the procedure and the reasons for termination.

The MTP Act was amended in 2021 to expand access to safe and legal abortion services and to ensure women's reproductive rights are protected. The amendment includes provisions to increase the limit for termination of pregnancy from 20 weeks to 24 weeks in certain cases, such as in cases of fetal abnormalities or where the woman's physical or mental health is at risk. The amendment also allows for the termination of pregnancy in certain cases, such as rape survivors, where the limit is extended up to 24 weeks.

Criminal Law (Amendment) Act, 2013 (The Anti-Rape Act) The Criminal Law (Amendment) Act, 2013, also known as the Anti-Rape Act, is a legal framework that was enacted in India in response to the 2012 Delhi gang-rape case. The Act amends various provisions of the Indian Penal Code, the Indian Evidence Act, and the Code of Criminal Procedure to strengthen the legal framework for the prevention and punishment of sexual offenses.

The Anti-Rape Act is an essential legal framework for preventing and punishing sexual offenses in India. However, the implementation of the Act remains a challenge, and many survivors of sexual violence continue to face systemic barriers in accessing justice. There is a need for comprehensive legal and social reforms to address the root causes of sexual violence and to ensure that survivors of sexual violence receive the justice and support they deserve.

National Policy for Women .The National Policy for Women is a policy framework in India that aims to promote gender equality and empower women. The policy was first formulated in 2001 and was revised in 2016 to address the emerging challenges faced by women in India. The National Policy for Women recognizes that gender equality is essential for the social, economic, and political development of the country.

The policy framework seeks to address issues such as discrimination, violence against women, unequal access to education and employment opportunities, and lack of political representation. The National Policy for Women is an important policy framework for promoting gender equality and empowering women in India. However, there is a need for continued advocacy and action to ensure that the policy is effectively implemented and that women's rights are protected and promoted.

Sexual Harassment of Women at Workplace (Prevention, Prohibition, and Redressal) Act, 2013. The Sexual Harassment of Women at Workplace (Prevention, Prohibition, and Redressal) Act, 2013, is a legal framework that aims to prevent and address sexual harassment of women in the workplace in India. The Act was enacted in response to the growing recognition of sexual harassment as a serious issue and the need for a legal framework to address it. The Act applies to all workplaces, including the private sector, and requires all employers to establish an Internal Complaints Committee (ICC) to receive and address complaints of sexual harassment.

The ICC must be composed of at least four members, including at least one woman and one external member who is familiar with issues relating to sexual harassment. The Act defines sexual harassment broadly to include any unwelcome physical contact, advances, requests for sexual favors, and any other behavior that is of a sexual nature and makes the woman feel uncomfortable or intimidated. The Act also provides for penalties for false or malicious complaints and for non-compliance with the provisions of the Act.

The Immoral Traffic (Prevention) Act, 1956. The Immoral Traffic (Prevention) Act, 1956 is a legal framework that aims to prevent and address the trafficking of women and children for the purpose of prostitution in India. The Act was enacted in response to the growing recognition of trafficking as a serious issue and the need for a legal framework to address it. The Act defines trafficking as the recruitment, transportation, transfer, or harboring of persons by means of threat, coercion, or deception for the purpose of exploitation. The Act makes it illegal to engage in trafficking, as well as to solicit or promote prostitution in any way.

The Immoral Traffic (Prevention) Act is an important legal framework for preventing and addressing trafficking in women and children in India. However, there are still significant challenges in addressing the root causes of trafficking, such as poverty and social inequality, and in ensuring that victims receive the support and protection they need. There is a need for continued advocacy and action to ensure that the Act is effectively implemented and that women's rights are protected and promoted.

The Juvenile Justice (Care and Protection of Children) Act, 2015. The Juvenile Justice (Care and Protection of Children) Act, 2015 is a legal framework that aims to protect the rights of children in conflict with the law in India. The Act was enacted in response to the need for a comprehensive legal framework to address issues related to juvenile justice. The Act provides for the establishment of Juvenile Justice Boards (JJBs) in each district to deal with cases involving children in conflict with the law. The JJBs are responsible for the care, protection, and rehabilitation of children in conflict with the law, and for ensuring that they receive a fair trial.

The Juvenile Justice (Care and Protection of Children) Act is an important legal framework for protecting the rights of children in conflict with the law in India. However, there are still challenges in ensuring that children receive the care, protection, and rehabilitation they need, and in addressing the root causes of juvenile delinquency. There is a need for continued advocacy and action to ensure that the Act is effectively implemented and that children's rights are protected and promoted.

The Prohibition of Child Marriage Act, 2006 The Prohibition of Child Marriage Act, 2006 is a legal framework that aims to prevent child marriages in India. The Act was enacted in response to the growing recognition of child marriage as a serious issue and the need for a legal framework to address it. The Act defines a child as a person who is below the age of 18 years in the case of a girl, and below the age of 21 years in the case of a boy. The Act makes it illegal to solemnize or conduct child marriages, as well as to promote or facilitate them in any way.

The Prohibition of Child Marriage Act is an important legal framework for preventing and addressing child marriages in India. However, there are still significant challenges in changing societal attitudes and norms that support child marriage, particularly in rural and marginalized communities. There is a need for continued advocacy and action to ensure that the Act is effectively implemented and that children's rights are protected and promoted.

The Domestic Violence Act, 2005 The Protection of Women from Domestic Violence Act, 2005 is a legal framework that aims to protect women from domestic violence in India. The Act was enacted in response to the growing recognition of domestic violence as a serious issue and the need for a legal framework to address it. The Act defines domestic violence broadly to include any act of physical, sexual, verbal, emotional or economic abuse or harassment by a family member against a woman.

The Act also provides for the establishment of Protection Officers and Domestic Violence Counselors to assist victims of domestic violence in seeking legal redressal. The Domestic Violence Act is an important legal framework for protecting women from domestic violence in India. However, there are still significant challenges in changing societal attitudes and norms that support domestic violence, as well as in ensuring that victims receive the support and protection they need. There is a need for continued advocacy and action to ensure that the Act is effectively implemented and that women's rights are protected and promoted.

The Dowry Prohibition Act, 1961. The Dowry Prohibition Act, 1961 is a legal framework that aims to prevent the practice of dowry in India. The Act was enacted in response to the growing recognition of dowry as a serious issue and the need for a legal framework to address it.

The Act defines dowry as any property or valuable security given or agreed to be given either directly or indirectly by one party to a marriage to the other party, or by the parents of either party, at or before the time of the marriage or at any time thereafter. The Act makes it illegal to give, take or demand dowry, or to promote or facilitate the giving or taking of dowry in any way. The Dowry Prohibition Act is an important legal framework for preventing and addressing dowry in India. However, there are still significant challenges in changing societal attitudes and norms that support dowry, particularly in rural and marginalized communities. There is a need for continued advocacy and action to ensure that the Act is effectively implemented and that women's rights are protected and promoted.

The Equal Remuneration Act, 1976. The Equal Remuneration Act, 1976 is a legal framework that aims to provide equal pay for men and women for equal work in India. The Act was enacted in response to the growing recognition of gender-based wage discrimination as a serious issue and the need for a legal framework to address it. The Act provides for the payment of equal wages to both men and women workers for the same or similar kind of work, and for the prevention of discrimination on the basis of gender in matters related to recruitment, appointment, and promotion.

The Act applies to both the public and private sectors and covers all establishments employing ten or more persons. The Equal Remuneration Act is an important legal framework for promoting gender equality in the workplace in India. However, there are still significant challenges in changing societal attitudes and norms that support gender-based wage discrimination, particularly in sectors such as agriculture and informal labor. There is a need for continued advocacy and action to ensure that the Act is effectively implemented and that women's rights to equal pay are protected and promoted.

V

Conclusion & Recommendation

- **Conclusion**

The laws relating to rape victims in India have evolved significantly over the years, with the judiciary playing a critical role in recognizing and protecting the rights of victims of sexual violence. However, despite these legal developments, rape continues to be a pervasive problem in India, with many victims facing significant barriers in accessing justice and receiving adequate support and compensation.

One of the key issues in the legal framework relating to rape victims in India is the burden of proof. While the law places the burden of proof on the prosecution, the reality is that victims of sexual violence often face significant challenges in proving their case beyond a reasonable doubt. This is due to a range of factors, including the stigma associated with rape, the lack of support and resources available to victims, and the legal system's tendency to prioritize the accused's rights over those of the victim. To address this issue, there is a need for greater sensitivity and understanding of the dynamics of sexual violence in the legal system, as well as better resources and support for victims.

Another critical issue in the legal framework relating to rape victims in India is the role of medical evidence. While medical evidence can be an important piece of evidence in a rape case, it is not always necessary or sufficient to prove rape. In many cases, victims may not seek medical attention immediately after the assault or may not have visible physical injuries. This highlights the need for a more victim-centered approach to rape investigations and prosecutions, which places greater emphasis on the victim's testimony and experience.

The use of character evidence in rape cases is another area of concern in the legal framework relating to rape victims in India. While the law recognizes that the accused's past criminal record can be used as evidence in a rape case, there is a risk that such evidence can be used to undermine the victim's credibility and reputation. To address this issue, there is a need for greater clarity and guidance on the use of character evidence in rape cases, as well as stronger protections for the victim's privacy and dignity.

The issue of compensation for rape victims is also an important area of concern in the legal framework relating to rape victims in India. While the law recognizes the right of victims to compensation, the reality is that many victims do not receive adequate compensation or support. This is due to a range of factors, including the lack of awareness about the compensation scheme, the bureaucratic hurdles involved in accessing compensation, and the inadequate quantum of compensation available. To address this issue, there is a need for greater awareness and education about the compensation scheme, as well as greater transparency and accountability in the compensation process.

In conclusion, while there have been significant legal developments in the area of rape victims' rights in India, there is still a long way to go to ensure that victims receive the justice and support they deserve. To address the challenges faced by victims of sexual violence, there is a need for a more victim-centered approach to rape investigations and prosecutions, which prioritizes the victim's rights and experiences. There is also a need for greater awareness and education about the legal framework relating to rape victims' rights, as well as better resources and support for victims. By addressing these issues, India can move closer towards a legal framework that is truly responsive to the needs and rights of rape victims.

· **Future Work**

There are several areas of future work that could help improve the legal framework relating to rape victims in India.

There is a need for greater awareness and education about the legal framework relating to rape victims' rights. This could involve targeted awareness campaigns aimed at vulnerable populations, such as women in rural areas, as well as training and capacity- building programs for legal professionals, law enforcement officials, and other stakeholders involved in the justice system.

There is a need for greater resources and support for victims of sexual violence. This could involve the establishment of dedicated victim support services, such as counseling and legal aid, as well as the provision of adequate compensation and rehabilitation services for victims.

There is a need for greater accountability and transparency in the justice system. This could involve strengthening the accountability mechanisms for law enforcement officials and other stakeholders involved in the justice system, as well as increasing transparency in the judicial process, including the publication of judicial decisions and statistics on rape cases.

There is a need for continued legal reforms to address the challenges faced by rape victims in accessing justice and receiving adequate support. This could involve revising the legal framework relating to rape victims' rights, including the burden of proof, the use of medical evidence and character evidence, and the compensation scheme, as well as strengthening the implementation and enforcement of existing laws.

There is a need for greater collaboration and coordination among stakeholders involved in addressing sexual violence, including government agencies, civil society organizations, and international organizations. This could involve the establishment of multi-stakeholder platforms for dialogue and collaboration, as well as the sharing of best practices and lessons learned from interventions aimed at addressing sexual violence. while there have been significant legal developments in the area of rape victims' rights in India, there is still a long way to go to ensure that victims receive the justice and support they deserve. By focusing on these areas of future work, India can move closer towards a legal framework that is truly responsive to the needs and rights of rape victims.

- **Recommendations**

Based on the critical analysis of the legal framework relating to rape victims in India, there are several recommendations that could help improve the situation for victims of sexual violence. These include:

Strengthening the implementation and enforcement of existing laws relating to rape victims' rights, including the burden of proof, the use of medical evidence and character evidence, and the compensation scheme.

Increasing awareness and education about the legal framework relating to rape victims' rights, through targeted awareness campaigns and training and capacity-building programs for legal professionals, law enforcement officials, and other stakeholders involved in the justice system.

Providing greater resources and support for victims of sexual violence, including dedicated victim support services such as counseling and legal aid, as well as adequate compensation and rehabilitation services.

Strengthening the accountability mechanisms for law enforcement officials and other stakeholders involved in the justice system, to ensure that they are held accountable for their actions and that victims receive timely and effective justice.

Encouraging greater collaboration and coordination among stakeholders involved in addressing sexual violence, including government agencies, civil society organizations, and international organizations.

Undertaking further research to better understand the challenges faced by victims of sexual violence in accessing justice and receiving adequate support, and to identify potential solutions to these challenges.

By implementing these recommendations, India can move towards a legal framework that is truly responsive to the needs and rights of rape victims and provides them with the justice and support they deserve.

Reference Notes

[1] Raj, A., & McDougal, L. (2014). Sexual violence and rape in India. Lancet, 383(9920), 865.

[2] N. Jagadeesh, "Legal changes towards justice for sexual assault victims" 7(2) IJME 108 (2010).

[3] Dr. B.P. Dwivedi, "Sexual Harassment of Women: Anathema to the Human Rights Jurisprudence" 1(1) IJLJ 1-8 (2010).

[4] Manika Kamthan, "Rape and Compensation: An Economic Analysis of the Criminal Law on Rape in India" 7(1) NLR 38-45 (2013).

[5] Indumathi M J & Dr. M . Suresh Benjamin,2021, A CRITICAL ANALYSIS OF LAWS RELATING TO MARITAL RAPE IN INDIA, Asian Journal of Multidisciplinary Research & Review (AJMRR) ,ISSN 2582 8088 Volume 2 Issue 5.

[6] Kamthan, M.(2018) Challenges in Enforcement of Rape Laws in India: A Feminist Critique.

[7] Rajeev Ranjan , Tanya Grover (2018) , Comparison and Critical Analysis on Rape Laws in India (Before and After Criminal Amendment Act 2013), IJCRT ,Volume 6, Issue 2 April 2018 , ISSN: 2320-2882.

[8] "Sakshi Rewaria (2019),Critical Analysis of Rape Laws in India and Judicial Opinion, International Journal of Reviews and Research in Social Sciences, 7(2), 298-304."

[9] Jhanwar, M. (2021). Rape Laws in India: Limited, Conservative and Devoid of Gender-Neutrality. Issue 3 Int'l JL Mgmt. & Human., 4, 1150.

[10] Chakraborty, A. (2014). Critical Analysis of Development of Rape Laws in India: From the Social Transformation Perspective. Available at SSRN 2402073".

[11] G.S. Bajpai and Shriya Gauba, "Victim Justice: A Paradigm Shift in Criminal Justice System in India" (Thomas Reuters, India, 2016).

[12] Pratiksha Baxi, "Public Secrets of Law: Rape Trials in India" (Oxford University Press, New Delhi, 2014).

[13] Dipa Dube, "Victim Compensation Schemes in India: An Analysis" 13(1) IJCJS 339-355 (2018).

[14] Michaela Lehner-Zimmerer, "Future Challenges of International Victimology" 4(2) AJCJS (2011).

[15] jhalak Kakkar and Shruti Ojha, "An Analysis of the Vanishing Point of Indian Victim" 2 JILS 313 (2009).

[16] Dr. Tiwari J.K., "Judicial Attitude towards Justice of Victims"49 (2014)

[17] V. N. Ranjan, "Victimology in India" (APH, New Delhi, 2012).

[18] Chakraborty, T. (2019). Law Relating to Rape and Sexual Offences in India. New Delhi: Universal Law Publishing.

[19] Jayakumar, V. (2019). Rape Trials in India: A Critical Analysis. New Delhi: Oxford University Press.

[20] Jaising, I. (2013). Rape Laws in India: Towards Gender Justice. New Delhi: Sage Publications.

[21] Kishwar, M. (2014). Sexual Violence and Impunity in India: A Feminist Perspective. Economic and Political Weekly, 49(52), 18-21.

[22] Kotwal, V. (2019). Exploring the Legal Landscape of Rape in India. Journal of Law and Social Sciences, 1(1), 1-12.

[23] Mehta, A. (2018). Rape in India: Legal Perspectives and Strategies for Change. New Delhi: Cambridge University Press.

[24] Mukherjee, S. (2016). Rape Law in India: Problems and Prospects. Journal of Indian Law and Society, 7(2), 139-158.

[25] Compensation Scheme for Women Victims/Survivors of Sexual Assault/other Crime 2018

[26] Chetankumar and T M Chetan Irannavar, "Victims Right to Compensation International Perspective", 1 APJR 178 (2016).

[27] Jhalak Kakkar and Shruti Ojha, "An Analysis of The Vanishing Point of Indian Victim Compensation Law",2 JILS 319 (2009).

[28] Chetankumar and T M Chetan Irannavar, "Victims Right to Compensation International Perspective", 1 SS 181 (2016).

[29] Ibid 6 (176-180).

[30] Government of India, Report: Committee on Reforms of Criminal Justice System (Ministry of Home Affairs, 2003)

[31] Jhalak Kakkar And Shruti Ojha, "An Analysis of The Vanishing Point of Indian Victim Compensation Law",2 JILS 326-327(2009).

[32] Chetankumar and T M Chetan Irannavar, "Victims Right to Compensation International Perspective", 1 APJR 178 (2016)

[33] Chetankumar and T M Chetan Irannavar, "Victims Right to Compensation International Perspective", 1 APJR 178 (2016)

[34] Vermeule, A. (2002). The constitutional law of official compensation. Colum. L. Rev., 102, 501.

[35] Jhalak Kakkar And Shruti Ojha, "An Analysis of The Vanishing Point of Indian Victim Compensation Law",2 JILS 326-327(2009).

Bibliographies

1. Indumathi M J & Dr. M . Suresh Benjamin,2021, A CRITICAL ANALYSIS OF LAWSRELATING TO MARITAL RAPE IN INDIA, Asian Journal of Multidisciplinary Research & Review (AJMRR) ,ISSN 2582 8088 Volume 2 Issue 5.
2. Kamthan, M.(2018) Challenges in Enforcement of Rape Laws in India: A Feminist Critique.
3. Rajeev Ranjan , Tanya Grover (2018) , Comparison and Critical Analysis on Rape Laws in India (Before and After Criminal Amendment Act 2013), IJCRT ,Volume 6, Issue 2 April 2018 , ISSN: 2320-2882.

4. Sakshi Rewaria (2019),Critical Analysis of Rape Laws in India and Judicial Opinion, International Journal of Reviews and Research in Social Sciences, 7(2), 298-304."
5. Jhanwar, M. (2021). Rape Laws in India: Limited, Conservative and Devoid of Gender- Neutrality. *Issue 3 Int'l JL Mgmt. & Human.*, 4, 1150.
6. Chakraborty, A. (2014). Critical Analysis of Development of Rape Laws in India: From the Social Transformation Perspective. *Available at SSRN 2402073.*
7. G.S. Bajpai and Shriya Gauba, "Victim Justice: A Paradigm Shift in Criminal Justice System in India" (Thomas Reuters, India, 2016).
8. Pratiksha Baxi, "Public Secrets of Law: Rape Trials in India" (Oxford University Press, New Delhi,

2014).

9. Dipa Dube, "Victim Compensation Schemes in India: An Analysis" 13(1) IJCJS 339-355 (2018).

10. Michaela Lehner-Zimmerer, "Future Challenges of International Victimology" 4(2) AJCJS (2011).

11. jhalak Kakkar and Shruti Ojha, "An Analysis of the Vanishing Point of Indian Victim" 2 JILS 313 (2009).

12. Dr. Tiwari J.K., "Judicial Attitude towards Justice of Victims"49 (2014)

13. V. N. Ranjan, "Victimology in India" (APH, New Delhi, 2012).

14. U.B. Roy Chowdhury, T.K Bose, & R. Prasad, "Rape: Its medico legal and social aspect" 30(2) IAFM 69-71 (2008).

15. Raj, A., & McDougal, L. (2014). Sexual violence and rape in India. Lancet, 383(9920), 865.

16. N. Jagadeesh, "Legal changes towards justice for sexual assault victims" 7(2) IJME 108 (2010).

17. Dr. B.P. Dwivedi, "Sexual Harassment of Women: Anathema to the Human Rights Jurisprudence" 1(1) IJLJ 1-8 (2010).

18. Manika Kamthan, "Rape and Compensation: An Economic Analysis of the Criminal Law on Rape in India" 7(1) NLR 38-45 (2013).

19. Compensation Scheme for Women Victims/ Survivors of Sexual Assault/other Crime 2018

20. Ellis, E. M., Atkeson, B. M., Calhoun, K. S. (1981) An Assessment of Long Term Reaction to Rape. Journal of Abnormal Psychology, 90, pp. 263-266.

21. Ved Kumari & Ravindar Barn, "Sentencing in Rape Cases: A Critical Appraisal of Judicial

Decisions in India", Vol 59, JILI (2017).

22. The new law now freed a rape victim from the burden of proving that she was raped and was not having consensual sex.

23. V.N. Ranjan, Victimology in India 83 (APH Publishing Corporation, New Delhi, 2012).

24. Chetankumar and T M Chetan Irannavar, "Victims Right to Compensation International

25. Perspective", 1 APJR 178 (2016).

26. The Department of Justice and Constitutional Development: Gender Directorate, Understanding the South African Victims' Charter – A Conceptual Framework (The DOJCD, 2008).

27. Jhalak Kakkar and Shruti Ojha, "An Analysis of The Vanishing Point of Indian Victim Compensation Law",2 JILS 319 (2009).

28. Chetankumar and T M Chetan Irannavar, "Victims Right to Compensation International Perspective", 1 SS 181 (2016).

29. Ibid 6 (176-180).

30. Government of India, Report: Committee on Reforms of Criminal Justice System (Ministry of Home Affairs, 2003)

31. Jhalak Kakkar And Shruti Ojha, "An Analysis of The Vanishing Point of Indian Victim Compensation Law",2 JILS 326-327(2009).

32. Chetankumar and T M Chetan Irannavar, "Victims Right to Compensation International Perspective", 1 APJR 178 (2016)

33. Vermeule, A. (2002). The constitutional law of official compensation. *Colum. L. Rev., 102,* 501.

34. Chakraborty, T. (2019). Law Relating to Rape and

Sexual Offences in India. New Delhi: Universal Law Publishing.

35. Jayakumar, V. (2019). Rape Trials in India: A Critical Analysis. New Delhi: Oxford University Press.

36. Jaising, I. (2013). Rape Laws in India: Towards Gender Justice. New Delhi: Sage Publications.

37. Kishwar, M. (2014). Sexual Violence and Impunity in India: A Feminist Perspective. Economic and Political Weekly, 49(52), 18-21.

38. Kotwal, V. (2019). Exploring the Legal Landscape of Rape in India. Journal of Law and Social Sciences, 1(1), 1-12.

39. Mehta, A. (2018). Rape in India: Legal Perspectives and Strategies for Change. New Delhi: Cambridge University Press.

40. Mukherjee, S. (2016). Rape Law in India: Problems and Prospects. Journal of Indian Law and Society, 7(2), 139-158.

41. Rao, N. (2015). Rape Trials in India: A Study of Judicial Practices. New Delhi: Sage Publications.

42. Shah, M. (2019). Sexual Violence in India: Understanding the Legal Landscape.

43. Journal of Gender Studies, 28(3), 347-361.

44. Shrivastava, A. (2018). Rape Law in India: A Critical Analysis. Journal of Law and Policy Review, 3(2), 129-144.

www.ingramcontent.com/pod-product-compliance
Lightning Source LLC
Chambersburg PA
CBHW040819120726
48005CB00012B/1464